There's music in all things, if men had ears:

Their earth is but an echo of the spheres.

—Lord Byron, *Don Juan*

ACKNOWLEDGMENTS

So very many people around the world have gone out of their way to show me help and kindness during this twenty-year quest for the big cats that it is totally impossible to recount them all. People from all walks of life, the humblest to the grand, from all nations and all professions and callings, united by a common appreciation of these magnificent and beleaguered animals. Bless you all.

Some particular people come to mind. Steve Turner, whose Mara River Camp in Kenya is a Mecca for wildlife viewers and photographers the world over because of its superlative viewing opportunities for lion, leopard, and—most especially—cheetah, has been extremely helpful over the years. The staffs at Sabi-Sabi, Londelozi, and the incomparable Mala Mala game lodges of South Africa were very helpful in sharing their unique leopard viewing with me. Fateh Singh Rathore, who made India's Ranthambhore Park into perhaps the world's premiere tiger-viewing opportunity during his dedicated stewardship of that magical place, provided valuable help. S. Deb Roy, whose directorship of the incomparable Manas Park in Assam is of the highest standard, contributed mightily by his special permission that enabled me to leave the boat and walk the fabled Manas River on the Bhutan border, camera in hand. Bhagwan Antle, who knows the tiger, and Ricky Schwartz, who knows the clouded leopard, have both contributed special insights.

The following people reviewed or commented on sections of the book. Their unselfish and generous help was invaluable and much appreciated. While much of the credit belongs to them, any mistakes are solely the responsibility of the author. **"The Cat: Supreme Predator"**: Dr. Melvin E. Sunquist, University of Florida, and Dr. John L. Gittleman, University of Tennessee; **"Tiger: Phantom in Stripes"**: Dr. Ronald L. Tilson, Siberian Tiger SSP coordinator; **"Leopard: The Super Cat?"**: Alan Shoemaker, Curator of Mammals at the Riverbanks Zoological Park, Deputy Chairman of the IUCN/SSP Cat Specialist Committee, and International Studbook Keeper for the leopard; **"Cheetah: The Spotted Wind"**: Jack Grisham, International Studbook Keeper for the cheetah; **"Jaguar: King of the Rain Forest"**: Dr. Louise H. Emmons, Smithsonian Institution; **"Puma: Athlete of the Americas"**: David S. Maehr, Florida Freshwater Fish and Game Commission; **"Clouded Leopard: Splendor in the Trees"**: John Lewis, Director of the John Ball Zoological Gardens; **"Snow Leopard: Phantom of the Heights"**: Dr. Dan Wharton, New York Zoological Society.

Alan Shoemaker, who wrote the foreword for this book and whose knowledge of all the cats, most especially the typical leopard, is encyclopedic, read and commented on the entire text. Alan is a perfect fit for the popular conception of a dedicated scientist: concerned, incisive, open-minded, informed. His patience in helping a floundering photographer, sometimes beyond his depth, through the highways and byways of some of the more obscure Asiatic cat races, can never be repaid in this lifetime. *Muy simpático.*

A catalogue record of this book is available from the British Library.

ISBN 1-85310-785-9

Published in the United Kingdom in 1993 by
SWAN HILL PRESS
an imprint of Airlife Publishing Ltd.
This edition published in 1996.
Published in the United States of America in 1993 by Voyageur Press, Inc.

Swan Hill Press
An imprint of Airlife Publishing Ltd.
101 Longden Road, Shrewsbury, SY3 9EB

Photos: Page 1, A wary leopard hunting along a strip of narrow riverine forest—classic leopard ground; pages 2–3, A jaguar (Panthera Onca) on the move; page 5, A clouded leopard (Neofelis nebulosa), the most arboreal of the eight big cats; page 6, A magnificent adult male tiger (Panthera tigris) lazing away a foggy morning in his beloved—and absolutely necessary—forest.

KINGDOM OF MIGHT
The World's Big Cats

Tom Brakefield

Foreword by Alan Shoemaker

SWAN·HILL
PRESS

For the big cat people of the world: Russians, Chinese, Sri Lankans, Indonesians, Indians, Nepalis, Europeans, Africans, North Americans, South Americans, and a host of others. Many are living proof that a committed individual, standing at the gate, *can* make a difference. They continue to soldier on, though beset with countless difficulties, even as the darkness gathers.

We are all in their debt.

CONTENTS

FOREWORD

MANY OF THE BIG CATS' FUTURE IS AT THE CROSSROADS OF CONSERVATION. SUCH AN UNPLEASANT

scenario is facing most large cats across all parts of the globe. While one can point to an occasional exception, most

populations are in decline, and without a significant change in attitude from citizens in most range countries, readers

of this book will have little to remember the cats by except pictures and zoos. ■ The pity of it all is that felids have

been an integral part of most faunal assemblages for thirty-five million years. From humble beginnings, several

distinct lineages of big cats have been identified, including the famous sabertoothed "tigers," sheath-toothed nimravids,

and giant lions of North America that survived well into the Pleistocene. Over time, of course, they all became

extinct. In the case of recent species, the cause was a natural phenomenon probably caused by widespread environ-

mental changes impacting most parts of the globe as the last glacier retreated. Regardless, no feline vanishing act has

been as dramatic as that facing cats in the twentieth century. ■ Prior to World War I, most cats and other wildlife had

little to fear from man. Firearms were rare in the undeveloped world, great expanses of pristine habitat remained, and

commercialization of the Felidae had yet to be conceived by citizens of the industrialized world. After World War I,

things began to change as modern firearms proliferated. And partially as a result of these changes, the last Barbary lion

of North Africa was extirpated in 1920. ■ After World War II, a watershed was unleashed on the natural world as vast

The lion (Panthera leo) faces the shadow of extinction in the wild within a human generation.

quantities of surplus military hardware became available to the undeveloped world. Not only were hunting parties able to travel into remote areas after cats, but they also killed off the seemingly inexhaustible numbers of prey species needed to feed these wild felids. And in a double dose, the end of this last great conflict brought with it the means to clear huge expanses of forest and other critical habitats. The beginning of the end for another cat was at hand, and the Bali tiger slipped into oblivion.

The post-war prosperity of the 1950s saw the emergence of a pent-up demand for forest and agricultural products. Couple this with advances in medical technology for both humans and domestic livestock, and it is easy to see why pristine habitat so necessary for the survival of large predators is now at a premium. As more people lived longer lives and required greater quantities of food to feed their burgeoning population, habitats for large cats began receding at an increasingly rapid pace. Simultaneously, technology forged ahead on the veterinary front, ridding vast areas of the tsetse fly and other noxious insects, all actions that benefited mankind but ones that planted yet one more nail in the coffin of large cats and other carnivores. In one example of this "success," the exponential growth experienced by the human population on Java, the mostly densely populated island on earth, is directly linked to the disappearance of that island's last three tigers in 1976. Less

well documented but equally sad is the quiet passing of the Caspian tiger from large portions of Turkey, Iran, Afghanistan, and Russia.

Most large cats made it through the turbulent 1950s. Unfortunately the 1960s brought a new curse in the form of an organized pet and fur trade. Worse yet, the United States was the world's leading consumer of this precious resource. As a plague upon the land, this consumption by Americans lasted until 1973 when Congress passed the landmark Endangered Species Act, which prohibited most large cats from being persecuted on a grand scale. In the same vein, this symbol of one country's perception of value of the natural world was not missed by others. In 1976 the Convention on International Trade in Endangered Species (CITES) restricted international activities by those countries forward thinking enough to ratify this treaty, closing down additional aspects of feline decline. As a result, today's organized exportation of large felids for any use is a fraction of that in the past.

A grim beginning? Yes. Is there hope? Perhaps. In most regions of the world, habitat destruction will be tomorrow's battlefield. Without the education of people at all levels, from heads of state to the simplest of farmers, destruction will continue because all countries have people to feed and clothe. As it stands today, many of the world's most famous parks are surrounded by a sea of humanity, all founded with the best of intentions but often estab-

lished without thought for the future. As a result, cat populations in many parks experience little new growth, the young being killed shortly after leaving their natal territory. More insidiously, corridors between adjacent parks are disappearing, thereby subjecting resident animals to the unseen threats of inbreeding. Although the immediate objectives involving reserve establishment are lofty, the long-term survival of its inhabitants will depend on the ability of larger species, and especially carnivores, to move between populations rather than die as maturity is reached.

Conservation is an urban word, sliding easily from the lips of New Yorkers and Londoners alike. Laws passed in the industrialized world are easily enforced; peer pressure alone helped reduce the fur trade to a fraction of its former self. Those living outside the West have more pressing needs; to them, tomorrow's meal is far more important than all the leopards on earth. These cats need worth. And some have discovered it.

Those fortunate readers who have watched lions in the Masai Mara sleeping off last night's dinner can appreciate what Kenya has done to conserve its cats. For that country, tourism is the number one source of foreign currency, and seeing a lion is every visitor's goal. In Ethiopia, the leopard of the 1960s was something to skin for export. Only later did farmers in rural areas link the plagues of baboons with this cat's demise. Now the leopard has a reason for being. And elsewhere in Africa, adding CITES protection to all leopards has brought a population of which may arguably never have been endangered in the first place to levels that various experts feel have expanded to as many as 900,000. In North America, mountain lions had no status prior to 1970 and could be killed on sight. Since then, this species has enjoyed a very positive reversal of trends affecting its larger relatives, or related forms in the eastern United States. Because of legal protection, this species is enjoying an unprecedented increase in both numbers and geographic range, and today (1993) only one state ignores its existence, the others considering it a valuable resource for all to enjoy.

There is still a long way to go. As this book goes to press, the Chinese have unleashed on the world an unprecedented demand for tiger bones that threatens all remaining tigers; in the event of shortages, all other large cats whose bones can be substituted face the same fate. Worse yet, much of the pent-up demand comes from affluent communities outside Asia where links to wild cats are slim at best. Do live tigers have value? Not for this group. For those who love cats as Tom Brakefield does, they certainly do. And because Brakefield has pursued big cats on four continents, his pictures and text will bring strong insights into why these animals should be preserved, and in natural settings, before this book is all that's left. ■

ALAN SHOEMAKER
Curator of Mammals
Riverbanks Zoological Park, Columbia, South Carolina,
Deputy Chair
Cat Specialist Committee, International Union
for the Conservation of Nature's
Species Survival Commission

Leopard (Panthera pardus), *skulker of the rocky ravines and riverine forests.*

When the last individuals of a race of living things breathes no more, another heaven
and another earth must pass before such a one can be again.
—William Beebe, American Naturalist, 1877–1962

INTRODUCTION

THE BIG CATS. SECRETIVE. LETHAL. ELEGANT. WHENEVER, WHEREVER WE SEE THEM, THEY BRING forth from us such a confusion of wonder, awe, dread, envy. They strike a chord. Resonate within us. Evoke an echo from beyond a distant hill within our innermost being. ■ Millions of years older than us and superior to us in more ways than not, the big cats are succumbing to us and the world we have built. A tragedy is unfolding before our very eyes, one of Promethean proportions. For the question is *not*, Can these wonderfully evolved, finely honed beings exist with us? It is, rather, Can we exist without them? Is a world that is so sterile, so poisoned, so crowded that even these consummate animals cannot survive it one in which we ourselves can long endure? Or one in which we would want to? ■ The tiger may well be gone from the wild within less than twenty years, followed not long thereafter by the cheetah and the lion, with all but perhaps the puma and the leopard departing from the wild within fifty years. ■ What kind of world will that be for your grandchildren and mine? ■

The cheetah (Acinonyx jubatus), uniquely blessed with speed, uniquely cursed with a genetic tragedy.

THE CAT: SUPREME PREDATOR

IF EDEN EXISTED, SURELY IT LAY ON TANZANIA'S FABLED SERENGETI PLAIN. THIS BEAUTIFUL savanna meanders northward into Kenya, where it is known as the Masai Mara. Vast open vistas, dotted here and there with striking flat-crowned acacia trees and rocky islands or *kopjes* (pronounced "copies"), beguile the eye and lift the spirit. The ancient Greek who coined the phrase "Elysian Fields" for paradise must have visited this place, for there is no other like it. Anywhere. ■ Huge herds of more than a dozen species of antelope thrive here. So do congregations of giraffes, zebras, Cape buffalo, and "Jumbos" such as hippos, rhinos, and elephants. This great and diverse stratification of prey supports an equally imposing pyramid of predators. From smaller to larger, there are eagles and other birds of prey as well as mongooses, jackals, wild dogs, and hyenas. ■ But the mightiest of the predators are the three big cats that have so far managed to survive here, in one of the harshest arenas on earth: the cheetah, leopard, and lion. So different, so similar. They live or die by dint of their cunning and strength, and must do it over and over again. For any of them, to falter is to die. ■ First, consider the cheetah—the most lightly built, weakest, and fastest of the three. This is the most specialized of the big cats and, at least within the narrow range of its particular prey, the most efficient hunter. To see a cheetah openly approach its target, then blur across the landscape at speeds approaching seventy miles per hour (112KMH), is to see mere flesh and bone make magic. Then the leopard, hardly

The puma (Felis concolor), one of the most agile of the big cats, needs every bit of its athletic ability when chasing such nimble prey as this varying hare.

larger than the cheetah but far stronger and more powerful. This cat makes its living in almost exactly opposite fashion—by stalking through or lying in ambush within the heavy cover afforded by the kopjes or small, narrow bands of riverine forest lining the streams. Finally the lion, far larger than the other two and a cooperative hunter that lives and hunts in bands called prides. To see big lions seek out and kill prey perhaps two or three times their own size is to witness struggles that at times approach the titanic. Truly, only a paradise could support such epic, yet tragic, central characters as these three big cats.

The cheetah can be found in open habitats throughout sub-Saharan Africa and, in extremely diminished numbers, in the Middle East. The lion, can also be found in suitable habitat below the Sahara in Africa and in a very small part of India. The leopard, making use of a wide variety of habitat, occupies a more extensive range throughout sub-Saharan Africa and much of the Middle East into Asia. This trio of lion, leopard, and cheetah makes up nearly half of the world's eight big cats. The other five are found outside of Africa: The jaguar and the puma (also known as the mountain lion or cougar) inhabit North and South America, while the tiger, snow leopard, and clouded leopard (the smallest of the big cats) range through parts of India and Asia.

These eight species of big cats belong to the Felidae family. Today biologists generally recognize thirty-seven species of felids, a number paralleling the dog family, the Canidae, which comprises thirty-four species. Familiar animals such as the bobcat, lynx, margay, and domestic cat, and almost unheard of cats such as the Iriomote, Kodkod, and Chinese desert cat, are members of the Felidae family. Supreme stalkers, these wild cats eat meat almost exclusively, their particular prey depending on the size, ability, and location of the cat. These most opportunistic of predators take as prey a panoply of animals such as elk, deer, impala, birds, hares, insects, snakes, lizards, raccoons, and even other cats.

Cats are transcendent athletes, displaying a lethal beauty and drama unmatched by any other group of land animals. Their paws carry sharp, retractable claws so they can bind to powerful, frantically struggling prey. They move lightly on digitigrade feet with only their "toes" touching the ground as opposed to plantigrade or "flat-footed" animals such as bears. Their flexible spine and other special adaptations give them an agile power that is the wonder of the animal kingdom. Because of their athletic abilities, independence, intelligence, and reclusive ways, cats have captivated and amazed us throughout all time. The big cats, most especially, are revered to a degree unmatched by any other animals except, perhaps, the canids. To see one of the larger cats go about the business of making a living in the wild is a supremely fascinating experience.

Practically every characteristic of a cat's body is related to the way it detects and catches prey. Why? Because cats have no option but to be efficient hunters. These animals, predators of terrestrial animals exclusively, battle for food in areas that have limited numbers of prey species that are themselves highly efficient animals. Furthermore, unlike many other carnivorous animals, cats cannot supplement their diet with plant matter because their digestive systems are specialized for meat. The larger of the big cats face the additional problem of frequently preying on animals larger than themselves, sometimes several times larger, and they must be able to strike down and kill these formidable adversaries while avoiding injury to themselves.

Observe a feisty house cat batting a rabbit-fur mouse, and you'll get a glimpse of how the big cats can dispatch their prey. Researcher Hans Kruuk, noted for his research on the hyena, found that a cat will either patrol its home range until it comes across potential prey or wait in ambush for prey to pass by. In order to do this efficiently enough to survive, the cat must possess keen senses so it can detect its quarry before being detected *by* its quarry. Then the cat must be able to conceal itself until ready to strike. Finally, the stalker must be able to move quickly and quietly in order to approach and capture its prey, and it must possess enormous strength to strike another animal down and kill it quickly and—for the cat—safely. All told, the hunt is a transcendent engineering challenge to flesh and blood, but one that nature, after millions of years of experimentation, has solved in equally transcendent fashion. This is why we so admire and envy the cat.

"Big" cat, or "great" cat? There are eight species of cats among the overall total of thirty-seven felids that are considered to be "big." Four of those are also "great": the lion, tiger, jaguar, and leopard; their young are correctly called cubs, and they have the special ability to roar. The snow leopard, puma, clouded leopard, and cheetah make up the rest of the "big" cat group, and their young are referred to as kittens. Facing page: One glance at the mobile, expressive face of this Montana puma (Felis concolor) amply indicates that this is a highly intelligent animal.

The tapetum's effect is prominent in this tiger's eyes.

THE SENSES OF A BIG CAT
Sight

Most cats hunt primarily at night or dawn or dusk, but they will also hunt readily during the day, depending upon the activity of their prey. The exception to this is the cheetah, which is almost exclusively a diurnal (daytime) sight-hunter. Consequently, a cat's eyes must be very sensitive to low light levels, and yet must also enable it to hunt during daytime brightness. Cats have solved this difficult problem through a number of adaptations.

Two types of light-receptive cells are found in the eyes of mammals. Cones are sensitive to high levels of light and are used in color vision. Rods function in low light levels and do not detect color at all. The eyes of cats, not surprisingly, consist primarily of rods. Another night vision adaptation cats feature is a layered structure at the back of the eye, behind the retina, called the *tapetum lucidum*. The tapetum is also found in many other vertebrates. This mirrorlike structure reflects light back through the retina to help produce a brighter image. Most everyone has seen the tapetum's effect, the eerie eyeshine that occurs when a light is shone into the eyes of a cat at night, or when a deer or rabbit is caught in the headlights of a car.

The tapetum is what makes night game drives, so popular at many of the private African game lodges, work so well. After sup-

per, guests climb into vehicles and go out into the bush on the roads through the park to view game. One or more guides shine very powerful lights up into the night at 45-degree angles (in open country) or more parallel to the ground (in thicker bush). The country seems to come alive with all manner of animals as their eyes are reflected by the lights. They were there all along, just not so pin-point visible during the daylight.

These night drives are more comfortable during the hotter seasons than those in daylight, and the landscape seems more remote, more mysterious, entirely different than during the day. Often it's possible to see far more animals at night, and the light usually does not startle the game unduly. The *crème de la crème* of the night drive is to spot the elusive leopard and, with luck, accompany him on his nocturnal rounds. In most areas and seasons this is a better way to find the leopard than relying on daylight game spotting.

Cats do have two different types of cones present in their eyes, though at a far lower density than we humans do. One of these is sensitive to green light and the other to blue light. However, it is likely that cats use these cones to see a wider range of wavelengths of light during the day, rather than using them for color vision per se.

The high concentration of cones in our own eyes improves

our ability to resolve detail during the daytime (visual acuity) and to see color. We exceed feline vision in both respects. However, our low rod concentration makes us very poor at resolving detail under low light conditions. Near the center of one of our eyes is a depression called the *fovea*, or yellow spot, which increases the density of our cone cells even further, enhancing our color vision and our ability to resolve daytime detail. Cats do have a broadly horizontal streak (the visual streak) near the center of the eye, where a high concentration of nerve cells leads to the optic nerve. This increases their visual acuity (daytime detail) horizontally, better enabling them to spot fleeing prey moving across this plane. This adaptation reaches its highest development in cheetahs, for it enables that cat to pick out prey fleeing across the horizon in the open country habitat most frequented by cheetah.

When cats stalk and strike at prey, they must be able to gauge distance accurately. This is especially true of the more arboreal cats, who must often jump from branch to branch with extreme precision. Consequently, evolution has given cats the most highly developed binocular vision of all carnivores, resulting in extremely accurate three-dimensional vision. It is so good that it is almost as good as our own binocular vision.

Another visual adaptation cats have made is the increased size of the eye lens, widening of the pupil, and increased front chamber of the eye—all to enhance night vision. Whether cats see "better" than we do is a moot point. They see differently, sacrificing daylight detail and color for better night and low-light detail. Our own vision rivals, in its overall effectiveness, that of any creatures on earth, including those in the cat family, the dog family, and the birds of prey.

Roaring—the Ultimate Salute from the Four Great Cats

Another well-known feature of some of the larger cats is their ability to roar. The roar is a distinctive, specific sound; it is very loud and resonant. Only four of the five pantherine cats are capable of roaring—the lion, tiger, jaguar, and leopard—but not the snow leopard. This ability to roar is what differentiates these four "great" cats from the other four "big" cats. Anyone who has heard this coarse, vibrant sound, especially in the night, will never quite forget the feeling it produces. The roar transmits an atavistic sense of the cats' lethal power, reminding us that the same sound must have produced dread and fear in our own ancestors in the dim past.

These cats have the ability to roar because of the structure of the bones supporting the larynx. This series of bones, called the *hyoid*, evolved from a part of the set of gill arch supports in the fishlike animal that was a distant ancestor of mammals. All of the roaring cats have a long elastic ligament, rather than an additional solid bone, connecting the other bones in the hyoid. The ligament on a lion is six inches long and can be stretched to eight or nine inches, allowing a much larger air passage and enabling the cat to roar. This ligament and consequent ability to roar indicates a close evolutionary relationship among these four cats. R. I. Pocock has also reported a short ligament in the snow leopard, but this species has never been heard to roar. The hyoid of the jaguar is slightly different than the hyoid structure in the other pantherines, and it has been suggested that it represents a more primitive condition than found in the other three cats. ■

Lion (Panthera leo) in full roar.

Hearing

Cats are able to hear over a very wide range of frequencies from 200 Hz up to 100 kHz, which is five times greater than the upper limit of human hearing, which stops at 20 kHz. However, at the end of the cats' upper level, the loudness or sound intensity would be so great that for all practical reasons the upper *effective* limit is figured at 65 kHz to 70 kHz, depending upon the cat species. This is still more than three times our own upper-limit hearing capability.

So what use is this ability to hear high-frequency sound so well? Rodents are a common prey for many of the cats, especially the smaller species, and, many of these rodents use ultrasound to communicate. This ultrasound does not carry far and is useful in short-range communications in dense habitats. Most of the rodents' ultrasonic communication occurs in the range of 20–50 kHz—well within the range of a cat's hearing, though inaudible to humans. Cats can thus hear the quiet squeaks of their rodent prey.

Smell

Although cats rarely use their sense of smell when hunting, it is still used as a very important method of communication. Cats employ their sense of smell among themselves, to both identify and to mark territory. However, the sense of smell is not as highly developed in cats as it is in most other carnivores. Canids' sense of smell is far more acute. Dogs and wolves have a far greater surface area of olfactory cells (called *ethmoturbinals*) than do cats (125 cells per square centimeter for dogs, compared to 13.9 for cats). However, the density of receptor cells on a cat's olfactory epithelium (a layer in the nose) is about twice as great as the density on a dog's, so that the net effect is that dogs have only about twice as many receptors.

Touch

Whiskers are specialized hairs that perform a tactile sensory function. This "touch sense" is extremely important to cats in varying ways. In carnivores, whiskers generally occur in four different groups: on the cheeks (genal), above the eyes (superciliary), on the muzzle (mystacial), and below the chin (inter-ramal). Cats lack the below-chin whiskers; it has been suggested that this is because they rarely need to bend down to sniff the ground in order to track their prey.

The muzzle whiskers are particularly well developed on cats. When sniffing, cats retract these whiskers against the side of the face; when resting, cats extend them laterally; and when walking, cats extend them forward. At the time of prey capture, the muzzle whiskers are spread like a circular net in front of the mouth so that the cat can judge exactly where the prey is for a killing bite. Since the cheetah is the most diurnal of all thirty-seven cats, and not only can it see its prey but also the more open approach to its prey, its whiskers are reduced in number compared with other cats'. Whiskers also relate to the forest origins and lifestyles of most felids: The cats had to travel through brushy, crowded places with a minimum of noise often in very low or almost no light, and the whiskers provided additional sensory guidance. Unfortunately, there is a strong demand for big cat whiskers for various Oriental apothecary applications, and this, in addition to the demand for fur and for use as food, encourages poaching.

Above: *The leopard (Panthera pardus) is one of the more nocturnal big cats.* Right: *Snow leopard (Panthera uncia). Even the snow leopard's high alpine home becomes quite warm on still summer days, and a cooling bath is always welcomed.* Overleaf: *A very rare "Florida panther" or eastern puma (Felis concolor coryi) with a deer kill.*

The Thirty-Seven Species of Cats

Acinonyx jubatus, *Cheetah*
Felis aurata, *African golden cat*
Felis badia, *Bay cat*
Felis bengalensis, *Leopard cat*
Felis bieti, *Chinese desert cat*
Felis caracal, *Caracal*
Felis catus, *Domestic cat*
Felis chaus, *Jungle cat*
Felis colocolo, *Pampas cat*
Felis concolor, *Puma*
Felis geoffroyi, *Geoffroy's cat*
Felis guigna, *Kodkod*
Felis iriomotensis, *Iriomote cat*
Felis jacobita, *Mountain cat*
Felis manul, *Pallas's cat*
Felis margarita, *Sand cat*
Felis nigripes, *Black-footed cat*
Felis pardalis, *Ocelot*
Felis planiceps, *Flat-headed cat*
Felis rubiginosa, *Rusty-spotted cat*
Felis serval, *Serval*
Felis sylvestris, *Wildcat*
Felis temminckii, *Temminck's golden cat*
Felis tigrina, *Tiger cat*
Felis viverrina, *Fishing cat*
Felis wiedii, *Margay*
Felis yagouaroundi, *Jaguarundi*
Lynx canadensis, *Canada Lynx*
Lynx lynx, *Eurasian lynx*
Lynx rufus, *Bobcat*
Neofelis nebulosa, *Clouded leopard*
Panthera leo, *Lion*
Panthera onca, *Jaguar*
Panthera pardus, *Leopard*
Panthera tigris, *Tiger*
Panthera uncia, *Snow leopard*
Pardofelis marmorata, *Marbled cat*

■

HOW A CAT CONCEALS ITSELF

Most all of the cat's physical attributes add to its consummate effectiveness as a hunter. The fur not only serves to insulate from extremes of heat and cold, but also varies widely in length, color, and pattern in order to help conceal it from the prey. The background color of the fur is usually similar to the color of the cat's primary habitat, but on six of the eight big felids, a wide variety of stripes, spots, blotches, or rosettes helps to break up the outline, blending the cat into the background. I have sat within a hundred feet (30m) of a tiger resting in a heavily dappled forest for a considerable amount of time before I spotted the four-hundred-pound (180-kg) animal. When the tiger finally did rise and pad softly back into the deeper cover of the forest, melting away like a wraith before my eyes, it was more like watching a ghost disappear than nearly a quarter-ton of flesh and bone.

In general, you can follow the shift in coat color and pattern as you move from habitat to habitat. Desert or semidesert cats have light-colored coats. The tawny gold of the African lion usually matches the golden grasses of the savanna. Then, as rainfall and vegetation increase, the background colors darken, and pattern-breaking spots and stripes begin to show up. These same predictable variations can be seen within a single species. Leopards from the desert are much paler and more lightly spotted than are forest leopards, and melanistic or black leopards are very common in some rainforests of southern Asia. The assumption is that so little light penetrates the heavy forest canopy that such a dark coloration may confer a concealment advantage.

THE BIG CATS: SUPREME PREDATORS

So there, *en passant,* we have the cat, or more specifically the eight big cats who, by combination of their strength, size, and beauty, are such very special beings: the cheetah, a supple symphony of fluid speed based on its almost divine specialization; the clouded leopard, smallest of the eight, and able to float through its treetop kingdom as miraculously as the cheetah moves across the open savannah; the leopard and jaguar, close-coupled powerhouses of the heavy cover who are blessed with a solid strength all out of proportion to their size; the puma and snow leopard, those agile athletes who can leap, bound, and turn so as to seemingly defy gravity's harsh hand; and finally, at the very top of the tribe, the two Goliaths, the lion and the tiger. What other animals combine such power with such grace as these two? What other land animal is so devastatingly lethal?

Each of the eight is, in its own special way, a serendipity of strength. Together they truly comprise a "Kingdom of Might," as I have titled this book. But theirs is a more honest, straightforward "might" harking from a bygone age. In today's teeming, high-tech world, which we have created and consigned both ourselves and all our fellow creatures to, they are so suddenly, so terribly fragile and vulnerable. Today, theirs is a might composed of porcelain. And if we break the porcelain, can it ever be mended? ■

This cheetah's (Acinonyx jubatus) spots demonstrate how effective camouflage is in breaking up the cat's outline.

Above left: *Jaguar (Panthera onca) in the rainforest.* Above right: *The lioness (Panthera leo) does the pride's major hunting and killing.*

The Patterns of the Cats' Coats

While it is generally true that the color of a cat's fur is similar to the color of its primary habitat, this explanation is also oversimplified. How do you explain the different colors and markings of leopards and cheetahs, which live in the same savannas with the lions? Once, leopards and tigers, and now-extirpated cheetahs and lions, inhabited the forests and cane fields of India. Some of these cats are patterned and some are not, and even the markings of the patterned cats vary widely. The rosette pattern of the leopard is clearly of value in breaking up the outline of the cat, but the solid spots of the cheetah and the stripes of the tiger work equally well. Why the variability?

George Schaller has suggested that the variations in markings also serve as recognition signals among the species. Thus, from a distance, a leopard can distinguish a tiger from another leopard. According to Schaller, this recognition serves to reduce contact and possible hybridization in areas where more than one large cat species occurs. This hypothesis is strongly supported by the fact that there is total geographical separation between the two sets of species carrying near-identical markings. The similarly tawny puma and lion don't live near one another in the wild, nor do the almost identically spotted jaguar and leopard.

Certain color details are often strikingly similar among the big cats, even on cats with different overall marking patterns. Many big cats (and other species) have some sort of white patch visible from the rear. Tigers have a white patch on the back of each ear, clearly visible at dusk or dim light. Schaller further suggests that these ear markings enable cubs to better keep mother in sight as they follow her. Leopards and snow leopards have a bright white patch on the underside of the tail, and cheetahs have a white or ringed tail-tip. These species carry their tails so that the last third curls up and the white tip or underside is clearly visible to any cat following.

Any parts of the body where the concealing pattern is interrupted are conspicuous. All the cats featured in this book have either black patches on the back sides of their ears, or they have white or light areas surrounded by black. Most of these big cats (except albinistic or melanistic forms) have white or light fur on the upper lip in front of the muzzle, and dark or black fur on the upper side of the end of the tail so that when the tail is lifted, it appears dark or strikingly marked to any individual standing in front of the cat. Researcher R. W. G. Hingston argued that these dark or black markings are used when aggressively signaling other individuals of the same species. He primarily cited the lion but generalized this argument to include other felids as well. Hingston noticed that normally, because of the position in which they are held, the black markings on the ears and tail of the lion are not visible in a face-to-face encounter: The ear openings face forward, and the tip of the tail is usually held low.

However, the positions of the ears and tail change dramatically when a lion signals menace. Hingston states: ". . . when he is angered he makes three intimidating gestures: 1) He spreads his mane (which is dark brown or black), 2) He whisks his tail above his back, 3) He rotates and draws back his ears. In other words, he moves the three parts of his body that bear the conspicuous colors. Moreover, not only does he move these parts, but he does so in such a way as to make the colors of these parts clearly visible to an enemy standing in front of him."

The classic and well-known gestures of an angry cat—ears laid back and rotated so that the backs are visible from the front, the tail violently lashing—are universal among all felids. The existence of these distinct markings, even on such a uniformly colored big cat as the puma, argues that these areas of dark color serve to accentuate threat gestures in most cats, as they seem to in the lion. ■

The Felids versus the Canids—the Grand Yin and Yang of the Animal Kingdom

The cats and the dogs are among the most successful large carnivores on earth. Each family exhibits a large number of species—over thirty—as compared to the bear family (Ursidae), which comprises eight species. While some of the cats' and dogs' survival strategies overlap, generally they have evolved classically differing strategies. In some cases these strategies are almost diametrically opposite.

As a general rule, canids are more social animals while felids tend to be more solitary in their ways. Canids frequently use this sociability to cooperate far more with each other in the raising of young and hunting of prey. The lion is the one big cat that is relatively social and cooperates to a large measure in raising young and to a limited measure in hunting. This heightened sociability of canids is why humans have found them to be such a flexible and successful domestic animal.

Individual cat species tend to specialize in catching only a few different types of prey. A cat, on average, preys on about four types of quarry, while dogs usually prey on more than six. Cats generally stalk prey or lie in ambush and then make a short dash of perhaps thirty to forty yards (27–36m) to strike down prey. Cheetah, the atypical cat, hunts differently, usually pursuing the fleet prey it specializes in for two hundred to three hundred yards (180–270m). This highly demanding method of chasing and striking prey has resulted in significant anatomical adaptations. Cats in general have small lungs that do not lend themselves to the extended exertions required by long-distance chases. They have retractile claws for gripping prey and a compressed muzzle with strong, elongated canines for stabbing into prey and severing the spinal column.

Canids are adapted for longer chases. Some, such as the gray wolf (*Canis lupus*) and the African wild dog (*Lycaon pictus*), can manage extremely long chases of several miles. Their lungs and cardiovascular support systems are extremely efficient as required by these extended exertions. Their legs are often relatively long in relation to body size, giving them long-distance cursorial (running-adapted) capabilities. Their muzzles are elongated, not compressed, increasing their scenting capabilities and making more effective the repetitive, slashing attack they generally employ.

The larger the prey that a carnivore can kill, relative to its energy expenditure, the more efficient the predator. Canids frequently hunt and kill in a highly cooperative fashion; thus it is not necessary for them to be as large as the more solitary felids in order to bring down large prey. The largest of the wild canids, such as the northerly races of *Canis lupus*, do not exceed two hundred pounds (90kg) in the wild; yet, acting in concert, they are able to bring down prey much larger than themselves—in some cases prey that is five to eight times larger. The largest felid—the tiger—achieves far greater size, reaching almost eight hundred pounds (360kg) in the wild, or about four times the largest canid. A single tiger can thus bring down large prey by itself. Cats can be injured or even killed

while capturing very large prey, as has been recorded for pumas, lions, and tigers.

The fundamental differences that distinguish most canids from most felids are legion and are fascinating. Cats have short digestive tracks compared to other carnivores, thus feeding more on easily digestible meat than on plant matter; other carnivores are more omnivorous. The behavior of scavengers is an interesting footnote on cats' feeding patterns: Vultures have been observed feeding on

Top left: *The maned wolf (Chrysocyon brachyurus), member of the Canidae, is an elusive, threatened wild dog that inhabits some of the same South American range that jaguars do. Bottom left: Many people are quite surprised to learn that the well-known hyena (Crocuta crocuta) is more closely related to the felids than it is to the canids because of the superficial appearance of the hyena. Above: Leopard (Panthera pardus) with an impala kill in South Africa.*

lion feces in East Africa but never on wild dog feces. It is believed that this is due to the low digestive efficiency of cats. Lions have a mean digestive efficiency for total food-to-energy conversion at 79 percent, with leopards being slightly higher at 81 percent. Dogs have a much higher digestive efficiency of 89 percent. (Incidentally, the vultures' own efficiency was 99 percent.) Thus, if other food is in short supply, the vultures can find additional digestible material in lion feces, but they cannot find enough in dog feces to make it worthwhile.

Researcher D. C. Houston suggests that because the typical hunting behavior of cats requires rapid acceleration and high burst-speed, they help to minimize body weight by having a short, light gut, thus minimizing inertia. In contrast, wild dogs (and wolves) hunt by sustained, long chases where inertia is not a factor; they need longer guts with higher digestive efficiency to supply sufficient energy for the extended exertion. ■

The Long Road—Evolution of the Cats

Tracing the evolutionary path of the major predators is a fascinating but frustrating process. The fossil records are highly incomplete, and specialists in various fields have disagreed far more than they have agreed in interpreting them throughout the past century.

Fortunately, advanced genetic research techniques within the past decade have given us far more insight and reasonable certainty about the genealogical identities of many of the extant species of big cats. And, although the fossil remains of the canids are more complete than are those of the felids (although huge gaps remain in both), great attention has been focused on the cats because of the special fascination that we all have for the cultural, aesthetic, and scientific attractions of the cat family.

Many authorities agree that starting approximately sixty-five million years ago (MYA), carnivorous animals evolved from primitive animals called *miacids* and formed two main groups: animals that had catlike features (known as the Aeluroidea, or aeluroids), and animals that had bearlike features (known as the Arctoidea, or arctoids). As time went on, the aeluroids and arctoids further evolved. Some species from both groups died off, and some adapted. As this happened, the modern families of the order Carnivora evolved.

Beginning about forty MYA, the Arctoidea further diversified into the Canidae (dogs), Ursidae (bears), Procyonidae (raccoons), and other families; while the Aeluroidea diversified into the Felidae (cats), Hyaenidae (hyenas), Nimravidae (or *paleofelids*, which are now extinct), and other families. The Felidae family (also called *neofelids* or "true cats") includes all extant cat species, as well as many extinct species such as some sabertoothed cats.

There are large time gaps in the fossil records of the existing neofelids prior to the Pleistocene era (more than two MYA). However, the development within the last ten years of advanced genetic typing techniques has allowed scientists to compare modern cats with each other and thus infer lineages in ways not possible even a few years ago.

It is now believed that the common ancestor to all the living cats lived fairly recently—relatively speaking—dating from about twelve MYA, and gradually the various species evolved. The ocelot lineage diverged from that common ancestor about twelve MYA. The ancestries that eventually sprouted the cheetah and puma diverged, along with two species of small cats, about five MYA, with the clouded leopard also diverging five to six MYA, followed by the snow leopard about three MYA.

The lineage leading to four of the five pantherine cats (lion, tiger, leopard, jaguar) first became genetically distinct two to three MYA. Paleontologists conjecture that the jaguar and leopard diverged from this ancestry more recently than did the lion and tiger and thus are more closely related to each other than either is to the other two larger cats. The evolutionary center for today's lion (*Panthera leo*) is thought to be Africa, and the earliest remains date from Olduvai, East Africa, 500,000 to 700,000 years ago. Approximately 250,000 years ago, the lion had spread to Eurasia; remains for the Pleistocene lion (*Panthera atrox*) have been found in Greece, Germany, and Siberia.

The oldest known leopard remains are from India and date to approximately two MYA. This was a primitive leopard that somewhat resembled today's jaguar. Leopards also date from one MYA in Java and one and one-half MYA in South Africa. Leopards entered Europe earlier than the lion did. Jaguars evolved from a leopard ancestor in Eurasia and spread to North America via the Bering land bridge and were larger and longer legged than modern jaguars.

Fossil tigers from Southeast Asia are known to date from two and one-half to one and one-half MYA. They seem to have spread over eastern and southeastern Asia by two MYA. Thus, about two MYA, tigers spread from their evolutionary center in eastern Asia in two directions. Tigers moving through the central Asian woodlands to the west and southwest gave rise to the Caspian tiger. Tigers also moved to the east and south into southeastern Asia and the Indonesian islands and eventually westward into India. Very little is known from fossil records of the snow leopard and the clouded leopard. The oldest known cheetah remains are from France, this was a giant cheetah, *Acinonyx pardinensis*. The modern cheetah (*Acinonyx jubatus*) appeared less than one MYA. The modern lion, leopard, and jaguar seem to be the final radiation.

Because scientific techniques continue to evolve rapidly, we are certain to keep filling in the mysteries of felid evolution during the next few exciting years. We cat admirers look forward to learning more about both the modern cats and the extinct forms so that we are better able to preserve the precious current forms. ■

Above: *A lion approaching a watchful giraffe in Kenya's Masai Mara.* **Facing page:** *Though not a "sabertooth" cat, tigers carry much longer canine teeth than do similar-sized lions.*

What are the Paleofelids and the Sabertoothed Cats?

The Nimravidae, also known as the *paleofelids*, which means "ancient cat," are an extinct, cat-like group of carnivores, many of which had features that we call "sabertoothed." The whole subject of the Nimravidae is extremely complex and clouded; some authorities even speculate that the paleofelids are more closely related to the Canoidea than to the Feloidea. Most biologists agree that sabertoothed animals have evolved in at least four separate groups, including both the paleofelid group and the neofelid ("true cat") group.

The best-known of the sabertoothed felids is a cat named *Smilodon fatalis*, of which many specimens have been recovered from the Rancho LaBrea Tarpits, located in what is now Los Angeles, California. This felid *Smilodon* is found only in deposits of the last two million years or so, in contrast with the paleofelids, which lived from two to thirty-seven million years ago.

The reason that most paleofelids appeared to be sabertoothed was that they possessed relatively long, compressed upper canines, which, in the extreme forms, were greatly enlarged and flattened bladelike teeth. The lower canines were correspondingly reduced, and the cheek teeth were reduced in number, also becoming bladelike. Sabertooths, as species with this appearance are often called, have been the subject of much controversy and an equal amount of fascination. Questions regarding the function and use of these huge canines are especially difficult to answer since no living relatives demonstrate a similar adaptation. Although there have been several detailed studies that have surveyed and analyzed the size, shape, and angle of the sabers, the shapes of the skulls and jaws, and the implied sizes of the cranial muscles, conclusions vary considerably. Some biologists have surmised that the elongated canines were used to stab through the hides of large, slow-moving, thick-skinned animals such as elephants and rhinoceroses that were plentiful during this period. The cats probably preyed on young and subadult animals of these huge species.

Other paleontologists have questioned such violent use of the saberlike canines, arguing that the canines could easily be broken by the shock of such stabbing bites, especially if one tooth struck a large bone or struck the hide at an acute angle. These scientists have suggested that if the sabertooths fed on carrion, then perhaps the sa-

bers were used for slicing the meat off the carcass. However, the massive forequarters and front limbs, as well as paws equipped with razor-sharp claws, would have made formidable weapons in the extreme. The large size of the forequarters and front limbs better supports the theory that these cats stabbed and

killed prey, rather than that they were scavengers. Others have compromised by subscribing to the stabbing and killing theory, but suggesting that the primary prey were middle-sized herbivores that would struggle less violently. Many of the saber-toothed remains recovered do exhibit broken and damaged sabers.

There were two main functional types of sabertooths, the dirk-toothed and the scimitar-toothed cats, with examples in both the paleofelids and the neofelids. The dirk-toothed types had long, slender canines with fine serrations on the edges. They had strong limbs and somewhat resembled bears in body conformation. They probably hunted by waiting in ambush and most probably were solitary. *Smilodon* was a dirk-toothed cat, but lived in more open habitat and may have lived in prides like today's lions. The scimitar-toothed cats had short, broad canines with coarse serrations and long, cursorial limbs. They were probably pursuit predators and lived in open habitats. Both types of sabertooths had retractile claws, which were probably very important for holding and subduing prey before biting with the delicate canines.

Two mysteries continue to puzzle paleontologists: How did the sabertooths use their massive canines to kill prey, and how did they feed themselves? Because of how they had to use their massive teeth, sabertooths had a much wider gape than modern cats have, able to open their mouths to a full ninety-degree angle as compared to the maximum sixty-five-degree angle of modern cats. Many odd theories have been advanced to explain the functions of these extremely elongated canines. One suggestion is that they were used as a "can opener" on the large armadillo-type animals. It has also been suggested that they were used to slice carrion, as a tool to grub for mollusks (as a walrus uses its tusks), and as a way of stabbing with a closed mouth.

However they were employed, these very long canines had to be used in a controlled way. A sabertooth could not have hurled itself at its prey and forced the canines into its victim in a frenzied attack because even moderate sideways pressures would probably have broken them off. Some have suggested that the long teeth were used in a caninelike ripping bite, which would have been used once the prey was subdued by the cat's forelimbs. In this scenario, the sabertooth would have used its forefeet to knock its prey off balance and then used these canine shear bites to wound the victim fatally in its soft underside. Neck bites either to the nape or throat would have been unlikely because of the risk of striking bones with the delicate canines. In any event, the long canine teeth would have been a definite hindrance during feeding. ■

Liger, a cross between a male lion and a female tiger, usually resulting in a huge cat larger than either of the parent species. This captive liger eventually exceeded nine hundred pounds (405kg) and was not excessively fat.

Cross-breeding between Cats of Different Species

Speciation, or assigning separate species status, is a complex and often thankless task. Obviously whales and penguins are two different species. But the wickets get stickier. Red deer versus elk? Grizzly bear versus European brown bear? One of the criteria that biologists use to classify a separate species is the animal's inability to hybridize—to reproduce with other species. But even that criterion doesn't always hold up. Reproductive isolation is not always absolute between closely related but separate species.

Natural hybrids in the wild between large species of felids are rare, if not unknown. For instance, although there is some difference between the habitat preferences of jaguar and puma, the two often overlap. (Puma inhabit the rainforest less than jaguars do.) Although there is a widespread belief throughout Mexico and South America that puma-jaguar hybrids exist in the wild, biologists have been very slow to confirm the wild hybrid's occurrence, and I have not been able to substantiate one. However, in contrast to the lack of recognized wild hybrids, large felids of different species in captivity are known to mate and produce offspring. Under zoo conditions, individuals of one species can become accustomed to members of another species that they would either avoid in the wild or never come into contact with due to differences in range. The best-known hybrids are between lions and tigers, resulting in a "tiglon" from a male tiger and a lioness, and a "liger" from a male lion and a tigress.

Generally matings between different species do not produce live young because of genetic differences. If live young are produced, they are seldom fertile at maturity, and are thus unable to have offspring of their own. However, the big cats are remarkable for the degree to which they can successfully interbreed with each other in captivity. Live young have been produced from the crossing of lion with tiger, lion with leopard, and jaguar with leopard.

The appearances of these hybrids vary. The lion-tiger hybrids are usually very large animals, generally somewhat larger than normal lions or tigers. The background color of the coat is tawny and lionlike but usually more intense in color, and it is overlaid with dark brown stripes. These stripes are more open and broken than in a typical tiger, and they sometimes form rosettes. The offspring of a lion-leopard cross is also usually large, almost the size of a normal lion, with body proportions more like those of a lion than a leopard. Often such crosses have a lion mane and tail tuft, but have the black rosettes and spots that are typical of a leopard. In addition to the hybrids between the more closely related pantherine cats, there have also been crosses between the more distantly related nonpantherine puma and the leopard. The resulting hybrid's pelage is typically pumalike in color, but leopardlike in its pattern of dark brown rosettes.

Although hybrid offspring of various species are generally infertile, Helmut Hemmer has reported that some hybrid females are fertile, thus making possible crosses between the hybrid and one parental species. Additional breeding of such fertile hybrids may enable researchers to answer various genetic questions about some of the big cat species. ■

TIGER: PHANTOM IN STRIPES

OUR ANCIENT LITTLE JEEP, PROBABLY ABOUT AS OLD AS I WAS, WHEEZED AND FOUGHT ITS way up the steep hill in central India. All around us clammy fog wreathed the trees like cotton batting, creating a fantasy-forest fit for a dinosaur movie, with one notable exception: It was downright cold, and little or no warmth came from the watery dawn sun on this midwinter morning. ■ Just as I was wiggling my frozen toes to see if they were still attached, we hit a particularly vicious pothole in the dirt track that was more crater than road. My head whiplashed forward as I careened madly to the left, and I almost lost the big camera clutched to my chest. Just before I righted myself, I saw orange liquid flow across the road behind me, followed by a smaller shifting pattern. ■ It was a handsome adult tigress, followed by her well-grown cub. She moved with a lithe grace and smooth perfection accentuated by the stripes boldly barring her side. Junior trotted along behind without a care in the world, as befitted someone protected by a 350-pound (158kg) mother carrying four-inch (10cm) canines. My first wild tigers! A dream of a lifetime finally come true. Quickly I snapped off a few shots that I knew would not work due to the low light; they were just for the sake of sentiment. The camera's whirring clicks did not bother her, nor did our screeching halt. She merely continued on her appointed round, melting into the bush as if vaporized. Certainly she knew we were there and were of no real concern to her; it had merely been prudent to let us pass first before crossing the road herself. ■ What I saw on that

The tiger (Panthera tigris) *is very much a water-loving cat.*

frozen, foggy morning was perhaps due to the conservation work of Project Tiger. Begun in response to an urgent call for tiger conservation by the International Union for Conservation of Nature (IUCN), Project Tiger was launched in India in April 1973 with funds collected by an appeal from one of the founders of the World Wildlife Fund. Because tigers (*Panthera tigris*) have the same problem as all major predators worldwide—loss and fragmentation of habitat—Project Tiger wisely took as its prime objective the saving of the tiger's habitat and thus prey species, not the saving of the tiger per se. Given a suitable place to live, the tiger is eminently capable of saving itself. At its inception, Project Tiger claimed only eight reserves, and tiger numbers officially were reported at fewer than two thousand—a precipitous decline from the turn-of-the-century's informal population estimate of around forty thousand.

In its twenty-year history, Project Tiger has given us several generations of these grand cats that have never been hunted nor, in many instances, even been much disturbed by people. The tolerance the tigress and her cub showed for our passing jeep is most certainly due to Project Tiger since the sanctuary where I saw her almost surely would not exist without it. Project Tiger, though involved in its share of controversy along the way, has been very successful in giving us a twenty-year respite during which tiger populations increased and we learned much more about them.

Somewhat systematic wildlife observation in India began largely after the British had been there for some years, intensively hunting tigers for sport, pest control, and, in the case of British aristocracy and Indian maharajahs, social status. The British officer class, generally middle-class types, hunted on a smaller scale for personal sport. The local Indians usually didn't hunt, though they were able to trap or poison some tigers that were causing them or their livestock grief. We now know that these consistently negative interactions with people had profound impact on the tigers' behavior. However, in those earlier and more naive times, people assumed that the tigers with which they coexisted were exhibiting "natural" behavior. Incidentally, this fallacy of equating an animal's "natural" behavior with the warped behavior the animal exhibited after long persecution by humanity was certainly not limited to tigers. However, since the big striped cats were the supreme predators located at the very top of the food chain, and thus potentially more competitive with and dangerous to man, the impact on the tigers' behavior was profound indeed. Now, because of conservation efforts, that has partly changed. We have made a number of preliminary but fascinating revisions to our assumptions regarding tigers. For one thing, though tigers do primarily hunt at night, we have found that they are far more diurnal than was once thought. For another, though tigers are certainly never as social as the lion, that most social of cats, they are quite a bit more tolerant of each other than had previously been assumed. Also, they are far more accepting of humans *when they are not persecuted*. Though tigers are never as easy to see as open-country savanna lions in Africa, we have discovered that, when located, many are almost as tolerant as a dozing Masai Mara lion. So much for the myth of the malevolent, lone, midnight-dweller seeking always to destroy any human who comes too close!

Since 1973, Project Tiger has expanded to eighteen reserves such as the Mundanthurai in extreme south India, and the official all-India tiger census of 1989 reports forty-three hundred animals. However, only a third of this number reside in the official Project Tiger reserves, while the remainder are distributed in other national parks, sanctuaries, and forest reserves, few of which are managed to the standard of the Project Tiger reserves.

Some knowledgeable wildlife specialists suggest that the actual number of tigers in India may be only half the officially reported forty-three hundred. These people have argued that tiger census figures are inflated for a variety of reasons, ranging from inaccurate censusing methods to the unwillingness of reserve directors to report a decline in tiger numbers be-

A foggy forest in India, a mysterious, eerie, perfectly fitting home to the royal Bengal tiger.

Present-day Populations

As recently as a century ago, tiger populations in India were estimated to have been in the forty thousand to fifty thousand range, with total populations including the rest of Asia to have been perhaps twice that many. Exploding human populations and catastrophic habitat loss in the twentieth century have seen these once healthy populations decline to perhaps two thousand to forty-five hundred in India and Nepal (about 230 of them in Nepal), with a total of from four thousand to seven or eight thousand in the wild worldwide. There are somewhat more than eight hundred tigers held in zoos worldwide with an additional unknown population in circuses and other private hands.

Ronald L. Tilson, director of the Conservation Office of the Minnesota Zoological Gardens and coordinator of the Siberian Tiger Species Survival Plan (SSP), offered some informed estimates of current tiger populations in other countries. Bear in mind that these estimates of free-ranging cats are speculative at best:

Malaysia: 500 to 600
Myanmar (Burma): 500
Thailand: fewer than 200
China (South China race): 20 to 50
Sumatra: 400 to 500
China (including both North China and Siberian races): 50 to 100
Siberia: 250 to 300
Vietnam: 200
Laos: fewer than 200
Cambodia: fewer than 200
Bhutan: 200
Bangladesh: 500

■

cause they might be accused of bad management. Research has demonstrated that the populations of prey species claimed to exist in several reserves simply could not support the numbers of tigers, leopards, and wild dogs also claimed to exist there.

There can be no disputing the fact that Project Tiger has been a success in many ways—in the short term. Tremendous public and political attention has been focused on the animal worldwide, and the tiger has at least maintained its numbers during this twenty-year period of decreasing resources for wildlife. The country of India, desperately poor and politically complex, has achieved a conservation success that many average people in the West can hardly comprehend.

However, this hard-won battle may be only a temporary respite. It is likely that tiger populations of fewer than fifty breeding adults (about eighty-five tigers total) will not be genetically stable over long periods, say one hundred to two hundred years and longer. For long-term maintenance of the genetic variation necessary for adaptive evolution, minimum population sizes of three hundred breeding adults (about five hundred tigers total) have been suggested for adequate species protection. Although some Project Tiger reserves have been expanded where possible, and corridors between reserves have been established in some cases, there is currently only one reserve in India (the Sunderbans in West Bengal) that approaches the population figure of up to five hundred tigers. The next largest population barely exceeds one hundred tigers total. Because every isolated population is vulnerable to extinction (for instance, a disease epidemic can decimate even a large population), species viability requires at least three populations that are sufficiently separate to be subject to independent fluctuations in numbers. For tigers this may mean a population of two thousand to three thousand animals per subspecies.

Thus, the long-term situation is very marginal for Bengal tigers, the subspecies that benefits from Project Tiger protection. The situation is extremely bleak for the Sumatran tiger in Sumatra. Other subspecies have far lower overall numbers and often more discontinuous populations—small, separate populations that cannot trade back and forth freely. It is not known if genetic viability can be maintained in the long term.

Some hope that extreme human intervention, including sperm collection, artificial insemination, translocation, and other means, will brace tiger populations, but these methods are enormously difficult and expensive when applied on a broad scale and in primitive areas. Without these interventions, however, we could easily lose half our wild tigers in the next decade, and it is quite possible that they may cease to be a viable wild species throughout all but their Siberian and Sunderbans ranges not long thereafter. Undoubtedly, if their genetic diversity is to be preserved at any reasonable level, it will take focused human intervention plus preservation of habitat. Many people believe that the tiger is the most splendid, athletic land animal alive today and that it is perhaps the most beautiful animal of all.

Project Tiger has made great strides in protecting habitat and saving the tiger. But, alas, this has been temporary. During the twenty-year span of Project Tiger, surrounding human populations have continued to increase almost astronomically, and this, coupled with exploding demands for "higher" (more resource-intensive) standards of living, has begun to force the tiger numbers to fall again in many of the Project Tiger sanctuaries.

Although Project Tiger's success has been laudable, authorities fear that it is temporary. The human population of India has increased enormously within the twenty-year lifespan of Project Tiger, and tigers are now rapidly falling back to where they were because of the inexorable crush of humanity surrounding tiger reserves. No less a threat is the severely increasing demand coming from "developed" countries for an increasing standard of living. Project Tiger's dedicated people who work at all levels will require much stronger help if they are to succeed. The above photo is the guest house at Ranthambhore, a Project Tiger reserve. Right: A fine adult coming to drink.

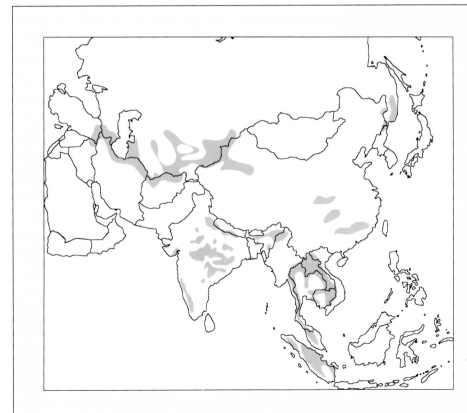

The Range of the Tiger
(*Panthera Tigris*)

When I was in Ranthambhore in 1986, Fateh Singh Rathore, the then–park director who had given—some might say sacrificed—his life for this great park, told me that the tiger population had been painfully built up to forty-four. But as of 1992, estimates had that population down to twenty-two and continuing to fall. Increased pressure from people surrounding the park who want to cut wood and graze cattle, and those who poach tiger prey outright, have conspired to send the tiger on a predictable and inevitable downward spiral. The same is happening in many other Project Tiger reserves, such as Manas in Assam. The tiger is the prime candidate among the "big eight" cats to be the first one to become—for all practical purposes—extinct in the wild. This could happen within as little as ten to fifteen years. Project Tiger has been a notable success, achieving all that could reasonably be expected of it and then some. But there are too many people. As Billy Arjan Singh, an iconoclastic Indian conservationist and tiger devotee, put it, "*Quo vadis, Panthera tigris?*"

The tiger is the greatest of the world's thirty-seven cats and probably the greatest of the world's land-borne predators. The larger giant brown bear is more an omnivore than a carnivore, being too slow to harvest any appreciable amount of its protein from large, healthy mammalian prey. The great white polar bear is an immensely impressive animal in its own right, but it can be argued that it is, to one degree or another, a marine animal. Also, although it makes its living by catching and killing large mammals such as seals and related prey, it does have a narrower prey-base than the great stripped cat.

The tiger is the largest and strongest of the world's cats, the most boldly marked, and, some believe, the most beautiful. No other land animal combines such size, power, and grace. It is an agile Goliath with the cunning, speed, and strength to consistently subdue larger prey, one-on-one, than any other land-based predator—an epic animal whose passing would diminish us all.

The cruelest of ironies is that this grand animal will probably be the first of the big cats to become extinct in the wild. If we save the tiger in captivity, it will be a singular accomplishment and one well worth doing. But even as we do so, let us be aware of the scale of our loss. We will have sustained an animal totally evolved to make a living based on its lethal cunning, but we will not have allowed it to continue to evolve in the wild, where its strength and cunning are tested and honed every day in the most demanding arena of all.

Muscles will atrophy. Instincts will soften and blur. Neuroses and atypical behavior caused by boredom will multiply. The king will still be with us. But he will truly have no clothes. One can hardly imagine a world without tigers roaming wild and free somewhere. Yet that may well be the case in as little as ten years. ■

The Outlook for the Tiger

Of the eight subspecies of tiger (*Panthera tigris*) that lived throughout Asia before the turn of this century, three—the Bali (*P. t. balica*), Javan (*P. t. sondaica*), and Caspian (*P. t. virgata*)—are now extinct, and the South China tiger (*P. t. amoyensis*) is in immediate danger of suffering the same tragic fate. The remaining five races—Bengal (*P. t. tigris*), Siberian (*P. t. altaica*), Sumatran (*P. t. sumatrae*), Indochinese (*P. t. corbetti*), and Chinese (*P. t. amoyensis*)—all have tenuous near-term existences, but can be in serious, if not catastrophic, straits in as little as ten years. Strong human intervention is required if these grand animals are to survive in the wild. The tiger, one of the most efficient and successful predators of all time, simply cannot compete with exploding human populations without help on a scale previously unimagined.

On the plus side is the fact that few other animals have been able to marshal such an army of dedicated scientists, political friends (Indira Gandhi stands out), and lay-person advocates worldwide. Resourceful work is going on in and between zoos to establish and maintain long-term captive breeding programs for the four most endangered races while there is still time.

Strong personalities such as H. S. Panwar, Billy Arjan Singh, Fateh Singh Rathore, and S. Deb Roy in India; Dimitri Pikunov and Victor Korkishko in Russia; Mohammed Khan in Malaysia; Boonsong Lekagul in Thailand; Charles Santiapillai in Indonesia; and others have wrought near miracles requiring unflagging energy and dedication and, at times, great personal courage. Special mention must be made of Peter Jackson, the tireless chairman of the IUCN Cat Specialist Committee, and Siegfried Seifert, who published the first landmark edition of the International Tiger Studbook in 1976 and who has continued to publish this all-important sourcebook from the Leipzig Zoo ever since. If the tiger survives into the twenty-first century, our children will owe these people and others in many countries an enormous debt of gratitude for that precious legacy. ■

Right: The "king" cat at his table. All tread lightly.

The Evolutionary Trail of the Tiger

Although at one time the tiger (*Panthera tigris*) was thought to be most closely related to the lion (*Panthera leo*), prevailing scientific opinion now holds that the tiger diverged from their common ancestor more than two million years ago. A later radiation in the family of cats saw the lion, leopard (*Panthera pardus*), and jaguar (*Panthera onca*) diverge from each other. Thus, the latter three species are more closely related to each other than any of them is to the tiger.

The modern tiger is unusual in that it seems to have always been exclusively Asiatic. It is the largest of all surviving felines—the Siberian subspecies has been known to grow to over seven hundred pounds (315kg) in the wild—and it appears to have originated in southern China as *Panthera tigris amoyensis*, the South China tiger, which is the most primitive and most distinctive of the eight recognized subspecies of the modern tiger.

Though possessing much larger upper canine teeth than the lion, the modern tiger is not a direct offshoot of either the fearsome "true" or the "false" sabertoothed cats, which are often called "sabertoothed tigers." These ancient cats lived from the Oligocene era (twenty-five to thirty-five million years ago) until as recently as eleven thousand years ago when *Smilodon fatalis*, the sabertoothed, stump-tailed brute, roamed the Rancho LaBrea Tarpit area within the current city limits of Los Angeles, California. ■

Above: *To witness the speed and grace with which a tiger weighing more than a quarter ton (225kg) can move is stunning.* Left: *A huge tiger can blend unbelievably well into any "busy" landscape.*

Physical Characteristics of the Tiger
Size and Weight

This largest of all the cats averages nine to ten feet (2.7–3m) in length, including a tail of about thirty-two inches (80cm). Tigers stand forty-two inches (105cm) at the shoulder, and the average weight for an adult, depending upon age, sex, condition, and subspecies, can vary from three hundred to six hundred pounds (135–270kg). Tigers climb trees poorly because of their heavy weight. There is considerable size variation among the five living races, and there are certain exceptional animals that far exceed the above parameters. At any size, this is a massively built animal with a rounded head carrying rather small, rounded ears. The tiger's belly does not follow the same outline as a lion's, but runs lower than the chest, while the withers are lower and the neck longer than that of a lion.

Pelage

The density and length of a tiger's fur, as well as its color, varies greatly by geographic region. The tiger's base color—the background for its stripes—runs from reddish-orange to reddish-yellow with the insides of the limbs being white or cream. The bold vertical stripes can be gray, grayish-brown, brown, or black with an infinite pattern variety. No two tigers are marked exactly alike, and even the two sides of the same tiger are asymmetrical in pattern.

Black tigers are known to have existed in Southeast Asia. But now the famous tiger that captures much of our attention is the white tiger. White tigers are not true albinos (which lack dark pigments), since their eyes are blue, not pink, and their stripes are either brown or black. The white background color is the result of a recessive gene, which can take effect when two carriers mate.

White tigers first sprang from "Mohan," an animal caught when she was a nine-month-old cub in the Bandhavgarh Forests of India in 1951, but at least three other strains of white tigers have now appeared. Although the "pulling power" of these strains in zoo exhibits and show business acts originally led to intensive breeding of them, there has been a considerable decrease in interest in these animals in recent years. Unfortunately, the inbreeding involved in building up the numbers of these white cats has had many adverse genetic effects, ranging from low fertility and disease resistance to eye problems.

Although a controlled breeding program involving both white and normal-colored animals could probably overcome many of these defects, allocation of limited resources and zoo spaces to this interesting but aberrant phenomenon, when the species itself is in such desperate condition, has drawn considerable criticism of late. Additionally, as Ron Tilson succinctly stated, ". . . outbreeding is the Species Survival Plan (SSP) philosophy; inbreeding is the white tiger philosophy." ■

Above: A "white" tiger, a beautiful but fragile aberrant. Right: A young Bengal tiger cub, about sixteen weeks old, explores his world.

The Tiger Subspecies
Siberian Tiger

The Siberian tiger, also known as the Amur, Korean, or Manchurian tiger (*Panthera tigris altaica*), is the largest of all the cats: A large Siberian tiger was killed in the wild in 1934 that weighed 771 pounds (347kg), another in 1936 that weighed 716 pounds (322kg), and still another in central Manchuria in 1962 that weighed 705 pounds (317kg). Captive tigers weighing in excess of 800 pounds (360kg) have been reported. Remember that the preceding authenticated weights for wild Siberian tigers have been reported during a period of extremely low populations. What the optimal size of this animal might theoretically be is something about which we can only speculate, but it must be awesome.

The Siberian tiger has a distinctively pale coat carrying brown rather than black stripes. In winter, the Siberian tiger's fur grows very long and shaggy. Its muzzle is broader than that of the other tigers. As with all tigers, males are considerably larger than females, and they grow a ruff of hair around the neck, sometimes almost approximating a mane.

In the late 1930s the total tiger population in the then–USSR numbered only twenty to thirty animals. Urgent conservation measures were put in place, and by the early 1980s the USSR population of *altaica* was estimated at over two hundred animals. The USSR performed a singular conservation service in this respect. Today, estimates of this population vary from 250 to three hundred.

As recently as 1974–76, 150 Siberian tigers were estimated to inhabit northeastern China. Tragically, this number has declined, due to poaching and habitat loss, to a dismal maximum of thirty to fifty animals. It is highly doubtful if any wild Siberian tigers remain alive today in North Korea.

The Siberian tiger is the most well-represented tiger race in the world's zoos, and in addition to the 250 to three hundred still in the wild, there are approximately 665 alive today in North American and European zoos, with an unknown additional number in Asian zoos.

Dimitri E. Pikunov, a leading Russian authority on Siberian tigers, believes that these cats maintain a two-to-four-times higher ratio of males to females compared with Indian tigers. The effect of a relatively large number of breeding males for the same number of females may mean that the Siberian tiger can exist without threat of inbreeding at lower population levels than can the Bengal tiger of India. A core of authorities dispute this contention of Pikunov's. However, if true, it would mean good news for the greatest of the great cats.

Bengal Tiger

Though the Bengal, or Indian, tiger (*Panthera tigris tigris*) may reach the same lengths as the Siberian tiger, it is less massive, and its coat varies from light yellow to reddish-yellow with black stripes. The longest accurately measured Bengal tiger, recorded in 1907, stretched ten feet, seven inches (3.2m)—of which three feet, seven inches (1m) was tail—and weighed a surprisingly light 491 pounds (221kg). A huge male killed in Nepal in 1942 weighed 705 pounds (317.3kg), while another giant, killed in India in 1910, weighed 700 pounds (317kg) and spanned nine feet, eleven and one-half inches (3m) in length.

However, all of these were dwarfed by a gigantic cat killed in northern India in 1967, which measured ten feet, seven inches (3.2m) and weighed a mind-boggling 857 pounds (386kg)! This is perhaps a bit inflated, as the cat had just killed a buffalo the previous evening and had probably eaten heavily. Scientist George B. Schaller says that a tiger can eat as much as 20 percent of its body weight in one sitting, meaning that, in theory, this cat could have eaten as much as 140 pounds (63kg) of meat. However, even taking this into account, the tiger might have weighed at least 715 pounds (322kg) with an empty stomach. Still a feline colossus!

It should be remembered that all of these really heavy Bengal tigers were confirmed

Where the Tigers Live

Tigers are basically forest animals inhabiting all types from wet evergreen and mangrove forests in India to moist deciduous forests in Nepal to heavy forests in Myanmar (formerly Burma) and mixed open forest in Indochina. Siberian tigers live in uninhabited mountain forests, where the temperature can average as low as -28 degrees Fahrenheit (-33°C) in the winter, while their Bengal cousins will frequently endure temperatures reaching well over 100 degrees Fahrenheit (37.8°C)—an adaptive animal!

Tigers are, except for jaguars, the most aquatic of the big cats; it seems this huge, northern-origin cat likes to dip into the water to cool down throughout much of its current tropical range. I have seen them happily luxuriating in a large lake in Ranthambhore to escape the oppressive heat. They are excellent swimmers, being known to readily cross wide bodies of water.

Tigers are primarily nocturnal, but in protected areas they have become almost diurnal. Tigers are at the pinnacle of the food chain where they live; they have nothing to fear—except *Homo sapiens*. Where we stop persecuting them, they tend to become more diurnal if the heat allows. In very hot weather, their prey tends to move more at night, and the tiger follows this pattern because of the oppressive heat and their prey's reaction to it. ■

Top: *Siberian tigers hunt wild boar, moose, wapiti (American elk), sika deer, and goral and roe deer. Since India has more species of deer (seven) than any country on earth, Bengal tigers prey heavily on them as well as on antelope, gaur, and wild and domesticated water buffalo. Tigers, along with leopards, prey readily on other predators and will, if they can, kill leopards and bears. (Bears, in turn, kill young tigers—as do adult male tigers.) They will also, if they can, take young elephants and rhinos, and will readily take peafowl, small rodents, and all sorts of other prey, being highly opportunistic like most successful predators. Here, the tiger feeds on a chital deer. Bottom left: The Sambar, largest of the Indian deer, sometimes weighing upwards of five hundred pounds (225kg), is prime tiger prey. Above: Except for jaguars, tigers are the most aquatic of the big cats.*

cattle-killers and consequently very bulky. The average adult male Indian tiger measures nine feet, three inches (2.7m) and weighs about 420 pounds (189kg) in the wild.

This tiger of classic storytelling once roamed forested areas of the entire Indian subcontinent as well as parts of present-day Pakistan. Today its greatly reduced population is restricted to small scattered groups in India, Nepal, Bangladesh, and Myanmar.

The tiger, along with the leopard, has the worst reputation as a "man-eater" among the big cats, and the Bengal tiger had the worst reputation among the tigers. However, it was estimated by no less an authority than the legendary Jim Corbett, author of *Man-Eaters of Kumaon* and many other classics, that no more than three out of each one thousand tigers was guilty of attacking humans, even in the most notorious area and era when Corbett hunted. Humans are not the normal prey of tigers, and the cats are not programmed to regard them as such.

The conventional wisdom has it that usually the culprit is a very old or injured cat, often living in an area of inadequate prey density. However, there are numerous examples indicating that these assumptions do not cover all cases. The Sunderbans is the largest patch of mangrove forest in the world, covering twenty-three hundred square miles (5,980 sq. km) in Bangladesh and an additional fifteen hundred square miles (3,900 sq. km) in neighboring India. This area (thirty-eight hundred square miles, 9,880 sq. km) holds the largest single population of wild tigers, about five hundred, left on earth.

During a twenty-eight-year period (1956–1983), 554 people were reported killed by tigers in the Bangladesh section of their range and slightly more than a thousand in the Indian section. As high as this toll is, it does not cover a significant number of tiger-caused deaths that were not reported for one reason or another. Tigers have always killed many people in this area, even though the density of natural prey (primarily axis deer and wild boar) is generally more than adequate to support them. Almost all human casualties have been adult males who were the last person in line when a group of woodcutters or others entered the forest.

In recent years, people entering the forest have armed themselves with boldly painted masks attached to the back of their heads so that they appear to be facing both ways. Though many authorities felt this solution, when initially proposed, bordered on the ludicrous, it has proven enormously effective, reducing casualties to almost zero when used.

At one time some researchers speculated that the man-eating behavior of the tigers in the Sunderbans was not correlated to the density of prey species but to the salinity of the water and the height of the water. Detailed follow-up analysis did not justify that hypothesis. To date we have not been able to conclusively resolve why there has been such a long-term, recurring incidence of "man-eating" by Sunderbans tigers. However, it has certainly been a fact, and these cats are justly famed for their animosity to people. It has not been due to lack of prey as there is plenty of wild prey in this area

and there has been plenty of prey throughout the years. Nor is it related to infirm tigers—as is often the case elsewhere. Just one more fascinating riddle relating to the striped enigma.

Indochinese Tiger

This race (*Panthera tigris corbetti*) was described scientifically as a separate subspecies only as recently as 1968. It ranges from the Irrawaddy River of Myanmar eastward through Thailand, south to peninsular Malaysia, and back north to Indochina and into southern China. It is smaller, darker, and less boldly striped than the Bengal race. Current estimates indicate perhaps 250 animals in Myanmar, fewer than two hundred in Thailand, and five hundred to six hundred in Malaysia. As recently as the 1930s, there were an estimated three thousand *corbetti* in Malaysia alone, but, due to the spread of firearms and the rapid opening up of forests for agriculture, mining, and human settlement, these numbers have plummeted.

South China Tiger

The South China tiger (*Panthera tigris amoyensis*), generally regarded as the stem tiger, is also smaller than the Bengal tiger, with less extensive white areas underneath and stripes that are shorter, broader, and less numerous. It once ranged throughout central China, mainly south of the Yangtse. Lu Houji of East China Normal University in Shanghai reported that in 1949 it was estimated there were four thousand Chinese tigers. It was roughly estimated that more than one thousand tigers were annihilated in the 1950–60 governmental "antipest campaigns" staged in the southern provinces. Numbers declined to 150 to two hundred by 1982, and only thirty to forty or fewer are in the wild at the present time.

There are approximately forty pure South China tigers currently in Chinese zoos, all of them captive-born and third or fourth generation captive cats. Unfortunately all are either descended from a single tigress caught in Fukian or from five tigers held in Guizhou, which results in a very limited genetic base for any captive-breeding program.

Professor Tan Bangkie, advisor to the Beijing Zoo, has stated that "the present status of the wild South China tiger is both alarming and disappointing. The remnant population is so small that there is scant hope of natural recovery." He added that the only hope for saving this precious subspecies from doom is working out a well-planned breeding program. There may well be fewer than twenty of these tigers left in the wild.

Steps are being taken to establish a captive-breeding program in Chinese zoos, but it is imperative that tigers be wild-captured to enrich the gene pool. A call has gone out for international assistance in this regard. If we lose this animal it will mean that four of the eight tiger races have been lost in the last half-century.

Sumatran Tiger

Smaller than the Bengal tiger, the Sumatran tiger (*Panthera tigris sumatrae*) is dark reddish-yellow with white areas much reduced and

Could a more spectacularly beautiful animal be designed even by a committee of artists?

more cream than white. The stripes are black, broad, long, and often double. As recently as 1978, Markus Borner of the Frankfurt Zoological Society estimated approximately a thousand of these cats were left on the Indonesian island of Sumatra. This has been reduced to perhaps three hundred to 450 in the wild. A zoo population of approximately 167 pure Sumatrans in North America and Europe (the number in Asia is unknown) establishes this cat as having the second-largest worldwide captive population of a pure-strain tiger race.

Charles Santiapillai of the World Wildlife Fund says that the Sumatran tiger has its back to the wall in several of its habitats. But the fact that it survives shows that it is adaptable as long as it has sufficient prey, fresh water, and adequate habitat. The problem is compounded due to the fact that the nearby island of Java has about 110 million people, and every year Sumatra receives about six hundred thousand people, so-called "transmigrants," from Java. Each year Java also increases its own population by two million, so migration is not going to solve their population problem. It has been estimated that Sumatra has lost 65 to 80 percent of its forests.

Bali and Javan Tigers

At one time, the Indonesian islands supported two races of tiger in addition to the Sumatran: the Bali (*Panthera tigris balica*) and the Javan (*Panthera tigris sondaicus*). These two subspecies were very small animals with males averaging only two hundred to 220 pounds (90–99kg), and they were even darker than the Sumatran tiger. The Javan tiger had numerous close-set stripes, while the Bali tiger was believed to have fewer stripes and to be the darkest of all the races of tiger.

Biologists suggest that the Bali could have swum the narrow strait, only one and one-half miles (2.4km) wide, separating Bali from Java. The Bali tiger was fairly common at the turn of this century, but the last wild individual killed was shot at Sumbar Kima, West Bali, on September 27, 1937. By 1963 there were only three or four left in a reserve in western Bali. There have been no sightings since 1970. Doubt has been expressed about the validity of the Bali tiger as a subspecies, although it has been recognized as such by science since 1912.

The Javan tiger was still fairly abundant until the early 1930s,

but by 1955 only twenty to twenty-five tigers were left on Java, of which ten or twelve were in the Ujung Kulon Reserve at the western tip of the island. During the 1960s the tigers in the Ujung Kulon and Baluran reserves were exterminated, and by 1972 there were only three to seven in the Merv Betiri Forest Reserve and another five in the Sukamati Reserve of southeastern Java. There have been no sightings since 1975, and this cat is regarded as extinct.

Caspian Tiger

The Caspian tiger (*Panthera tigris virgata*) was about the same size as the Bengal tiger, and its coat color was similar, but the stripes were lighter, longer, more narrow, and set more closely together. The hair on the back of its neck could form a slight mane. This was the westernmost tiger, reaching all the way to eastern Turkey in Asia Minor and inhabiting vast stretches of territory in Iran, northern Iraq, Afghanistan, and on both sides of the Caspian Sea in what was once the USSR. No recent trace has been found, and this race has almost surely become extinct within the last fifteen years. ∎

Left: *Find water, and you often find the tiger.* Above: *These young tigers, about six weeks old, will increase their weight about sixty times within four to five years.*

LION:
SOCIABLE SIMBA

IT HAD BEEN A FINE, BALMY MORNING FILLED WITH DELIGHTFUL SCENES OF A MOTHER CHEETAH relaxing and playing with her two half-grown cubs. In my vehicle I had eased around among them, slowly at first but with increasing confidence and acceptance on both sides as the morning drew on, finally photographing and observing them at will. It was late in 1988 in Kenya's fabled Masai Mara Game Reserve and definitely a good time to be alive—one of those marvelous days when things *do* work out, fitting the popular conception of a day in the life of a wildlife photographer. ■ Suddenly, as if turning a switch, mother cheetah snapped from supple relaxation to rigid, head-up alertness. She moved forward, literally quivering, a tentative step at a time as she stared into the high grass in front of us. Even from my elevated perch in the vehicle, I could not see what had aroused her. ■ Then slowly, ever so s-l-o-w-l-y, two small, closely spaced dots levitated above the grassline about seventy-five yards (67.5m) away. As they grew, I finally resolved what the dots were: the ears of an adult lioness peering intently at the cheetahs. Instantly the mother cheetah flashed forward directly toward the thrice-larger cat, closing to a scant fifteen feet (4.5m) before dashing off, leading the lion away from her curious cubs. The lioness exploded after the much smaller cat, pulling to within six feet (1.8m) of her before the cheetah cut inside and turned on that justly famed afterburner. The lioness quit the chase after running less than a hundred yards (90m), practically shaking her head in disgust. ■

One look at that noble visage tells you instantly why the lion (Panthera leo) is so often associated with the word "king."

This fascinating wildlife drama was repeated half a dozen times in the next thirty minutes. The lioness knew very well that those cubs were there and were vulnerable. But each time she moved toward them, the desperate mother cheetah would intercept her, dashing so tantalizingly close that the lioness's strike reflex would be triggered and off the two would madly dash, stringing puffballs of dust across the open plain. Gradually the cheetah drew the lioness further away from the cubs, and, as the heavier cat tired, the cheetah would have to dash closer and closer in order to trigger an ever-shorter charge. Finally the lioness tired of what had become a farce and moved off in a thoroughly grumpy, flat-footed fashion. The spotted cat squeaked, calling her now-hiding cubs back to her, and they moved off in the opposite direction, leaving me to contemplate all that I had been privileged to see. I thought of the research I had become familiar with: This midday occurrence was not unusual for these two most diurnal of all big cats. Also, the lioness's persistent interest in the cheetah came as no surprise since lions will, along with leopards and tigers, readily stalk and kill other predators, though they do not then consume them as do the latter two cats.

The cheetah's desperate and, this time successful ploy to save her cubs also certainly reflected her place at the bottom of the major-predator pecking order, which can cause a cheetah to be attacked and driven off kills not only by lions but also by leopards, hyenas, and wild dogs. I have even wondered whether a group of aggressive jackals, given the right circumstances, might conceivably harry the high-strung cheetah into simply giving up a kill in order to escape from a highly visible commotion that had a good probability of drawing other, still larger predators.

Most of all, this situation emphasized that the lion sits very firmly at the top of the African food chain, challenged only by bands of hyenas when the lion is aged and infirm. It is said that lions show such intense hatred of hyenas because they seem to instinctively know that all too many of them will eventually wind up in the belly of old *fisi*.

RECENT RESEARCH

Although the lion (*Panthera leo*), along with the tiger and the puma, is the most thoroughly studied of the big cats, there is a terrific irony in the nature of these studies. Practically all of them until very recently were strictly behavioral, due both to the complex and fascinating social nature of lions (which is unlike that of any other felid), and also to the complacent feeling that lion numbers were so great that strong management was not needed. However, almost everyone now agrees that more distribution studies, population estimates, and other management tools are greatly needed to curb the lion's current rapid decline throughout most of its present, much-restricted range. It is vexing that far more is known about tiger numbers than is known about lion numbers, even though the tiger is a heavy-cover, more secretive animal. Currently some studies are underway to partially remedy this situation, and some progress has been made using sophisticated computer-modeling techniques to extrapolate population numbers and densities for certain large areas where outright censusing is not feasible.

To date, most management emphasis has been on the Asian lion (also called the Indian lion) because of its far smaller numbers (approximately 260, as compared to the African lion, which numbers at least 6,100) and because of its vastly more constricted range. However, the lions of Etosha Park in the southwestern African nation of Namibia have also been strongly managed in order to stabilize lion populations. This is the densest lion population in the world, largely due to several artificial factors such as new bore holes for water and recent large die-offs of prey animals due to anthrax, creating easy scavenging. This has led to lion numbers that are out of balance with normal prey population densities.

Contraceptive injections and implants have been used with relative effectiveness in Etosha and in many populations of captive lions and other captive big cats around the world. The treatments inhibit ovulation and can remain effective for two to four years. In Etosha, all treated

Kruger National Park, shown in these photos, is a long ribbon of territory in extreme eastern South Africa bordering Mozambique to the east and Zimbabwe to the north. A country within a country, "the Kruger" is a fascinating story all its own. The second oldest national park in the world after Yellowstone in the United States, it is far and away the most scientifically and intensively managed large park in the world. The bottom left photo is the park headquarters.

lionesses were monitored, both medically and behaviorally, to note any changes that might affect pride structure. The technique is said to have become so refined that the research team is able to reduce population by a predetermined percentage.

There are different types of long-term implants in use. It does appear that a higher incidence of ovarian, cervical, and mammary cancers are showing up in captive populations of older lionesses who have carried contraceptive implants over an extended period. To date, no conclusions can be drawn since none of the disciplined, rigorous studies underway have been completed. However, the results of these studies may have far-reaching effects on the management of many popular zoo species of all types, from carnivores to herbivores, that tend to overpopulate the limited spaces available.

THE LION'S POPULATION

There are some very informal population estimates for wild lions. The only remaining Asiatic lions (*Panthera leo persica*) are in a small relict population of about 260 in the Gir Forest of western India. Two members of the International Union for the Conservation of Nature (IUCN) Cat Specialist Committee, Vivian Wilson and Chris Stuart, estimated the 1988 total African lion (*Panthera leo leo*) population in southern Africa, south of the Zambezi River, at between 6,100 and 9,100, of which about 4,200 are already in reserves. Exploding human populations are such

that there are no realistic prospects for the establishment of any additional large reserves in either Africa and India, yet there is no future for the lion outside of conservation areas. Of the overall population of African lions in southern Africa, there are approximately three hundred lions in Etosha Park in the southwestern country of Namibia; somewhat more than one thousand in Zimbabwe, of which about five hundred reside in Hwange National Park; several hundred in South Africa, of which most are found in Kruger National Park; and additional scattered populations in Botswana and elsewhere, including one thousand to two thousand lions in Mozambique.

Currently it is estimated that several thousand lions are left in East Africa, with much of the population currently being unpersecuted and thus reasonably stable. This number is likely to decline with the inevitable spread of agriculture. Due to the steadily diminishing prey base, domestic livestock depredations by lions are anticipated to increase greatly in the 1990s. Kenya's wildlife populations are largely supported by the tourism industry, which is fickle at best, being subject to all sorts of changes in travel taste and style and always responsive to the state of foreign affairs and foreign economies fueling this expensive travel. Tanzania has had some success with inculcating the more difficult but stable concept that wildlife should be preserved primarily because it is a national heritage and that tourism income is merely an added bonus.

Evolution of the Lion

The earliest known ancestor of these cats had both lionlike features and tigerlike features and roamed East Africa about two million years ago. The oldest true lions—ancestors of today's lion—are the famous European cave lions, possibly the largest felids that ever lived. They can be dated back six hundred thousand years. These older cave lions are frequently recognized as a distinct species (*Panthera spelaea*), while some argue that the more recent cave lion (up to three hundred thousand years old) is so lionlike that it should be called *Panthera leo spelaea*, a subspecies of the modern lion.

The older cave lions were up to 25 percent larger than recent lions or tigers in skull length, teeth size, and limb length. In addition to being larger overall, the cave lion's limbs were proportionately more robust, possibly indicating a larger than 25 percent increase in weight. The average size of the European cave lion decreased through the Pleistocene, until it was only 8 to 10 percent larger than the current lion. This lion clearly coexisted with humans, since we find drawings of these lions on the walls of caves in which humans lived. It has been suggested that the lions living in present-day Yugoslavia and Asia Minor as recently as 300 B.C. may have been *Panthera leo spelaea*, although there have been no skeletal remains to confirm this. Similar or identical cave lion skeletons have been found in Siberia, China, and throughout most of Europe, though the contemporaneous lion in Africa appears to have been smaller.

North America once had its own giant lion, *Panthera atrox*, which also exceeded the current lion's size by about 25 percent and had a much more massive skull. Some scientists have further speculated that this was a "small-headed" lion, thus implying an even larger overall size differential when compared with modern lions. Many scientists feel that *Panthera atrox* should actually be considered a subspecies of the modern lion, *Panthera leo*. These big lions existed in North America until as recently as 11,580 years ago, judging from remains found in the Beaverhead Mountains of Idaho.

It has been demonstrated that a relationship exists between brain size and the amount of sociality in carnivores. Recent lions have relatively large brains, and *Panthera atrox* had even a slightly larger brain, strongly suggesting that these animals formed social prides as do current African and Asian lions. By contrast, the sabertoothed cat, *Smilodon fatalis*, which lived during the same period as *Panthera atrox*, had a relatively small brain, about the size of the nonsocial species of puma, jaguar, and leopard. Earlier extinctions of these lions in North America, Europe, and most of Asia several thousand years ago may have been caused by a variety of factors, ranging from human persecution and hunting (in Eurasia) to climate changes (in all areas). We do not know how much weight to give these and other factors. However, later extinctions such as those in southernmost Africa, northern Africa, and most of India were clearly the result of relentless hunting by humans, and the continuing decrease in lion populations is due to assorted human pressures, ranging from hunting to habitat encroachment and degradation. ■

Left: The word simba comes from the Swahili language, which is a combination of Bantu and Arabic used throughout East Africa and surrounding areas and reflecting the long Arab trading past with East Africa and the Horn of Africa. The word means "lion," and implies king, strong, aggressive—everything that a lion is. Facing page: The king and his consort hardly five minutes after breeding on a pristine morning in the Masai Mara.

THE OUTLOOK FOR THIS LARGE PREDATOR

Lions share the same problems with all major predators in today's world, particularly the tiger. Both are simply too large and competitive with humans to coexist, except in totally protected reserves in the future. Even then, many reserves are not large enough to be fully viable ecosystems able to support the number of prey and predators necessary to maintain sound genetic populations of the big cats over the long term.

Even those reserves that are large enough and offer a viable, year-round ecosystem will come under ever-increasing pressure as human populations and their consequent need for food explode. Concomitant demands for an increased standard of living will serve as an additional multiplier. This demand for more land by agriculture and industry will continue to erode wildlife habitat. Political instability in many areas where lions are still found adds to these vexing questions about the future for the big cats. Kenya,

relatively stable by African standards, currently boasts the fastest human population growth in the world at 4 percent per year. Obviously this cannot continue without totally changing the face of the country.

More wild lions than wild tigers exist in the world, and there are more large and genetically viable populations of lions, so the near future of lions is perhaps a bit brighter, speaking strictly in relative terms. However, mid- to long-term prospects in the wild are not promising. Though the lion's current geographic range and numbers may appear fairly robust compared to the even more miserable plight of many other large predators, they are a sad remnant indeed of what was once one of the most widespread, large land carnivores ever known.

The lion and the tiger truly represent the twin peaks of both felid evolution and predator evolution. They are the largest and most deadly pair in that most lethal of tribes. Words like "lionhearted" and "lionize" and a host of others show the impact that

this lordly beast has had upon the human consciousness down through the centuries.

And yet, and yet. I well remember sweltering and broiling as I sat for seven hours under the burning Botswana sun in a Landrover hot enough to fry eggs on. Harry Cantle, gentleman extraordinaire and for many years on the park staff of that lion heaven, Hwange National Park in Zimbabwe, was my engaging companion during the ordeal. We had decided to wait beside a smallish pride of perhaps eight or ten lions to see what might eventually transpire after their midday siesta. We sat, sweated, and generally questioned our sanity. Black cameras burned into any flesh that they touched. Literally.

After many hours a herd of about twenty impala fed their way toward us, undoubtedly crazed by the tropic sun or they would have been lying down somewhere in the shade. Closer and closer they came as I had visions of photographic sugar plums dancing in my fevered brain. Now they were within a mere twenty feet (6m)

of us, less that fifteen feet (4.5km) from what appeared to be the alpha lioness. Finally said queen of the savanna raised her head, groggily contemplated the oncoming antelope, and flopped back to earth with an audible sigh and tail swish. The antelope came to their senses and madly stampeded away. I coolly considered my odds for survival if I tried to strangle this adult lioness who had just broken my heart. "Makes you wonder how the bloody buggers make a living," muttered Harry.

But they do make a living—grandly and gloriously in one of the harshest, most unforgiving fashions imaginable. When we let them, that is. Sadly, it appears that they—in a close race with the cheetah—will probably follow the tiger into extinction in the wild within a bare twenty years or less.

How does that speak to *Homo sapiens* with our inexorable appetites, our inevitable follies, our wretched excesses? Will we be "lionhearted" or worthy of being "lionized" when *Panthera leo* is but a dim memory of a past grandeur? ∎

Above: In places where the three overlap, lions, leopards, and cheetahs often interact. Leopards can handle lions quite well because they can climb trees to escape the larger cat. Also, leopards can rescue their threatened young, or at least one of them, by taking them up a tree. The leopard can also pull its kills up into trees to protect them from lions. It is the cheetahs that lions can really decimate, given enough lion density and competition for similar prey. Cheetahs can climb a little to escape danger, but not much. Given the right tree, a lion can climb about as well. More to the point for the cheetah: Lions hunt cheetahs to kill their kittens, and cheetahs cannot save their kills from either lions or leopards. Here, a lioness chases a cheetah. Left: A lion at a kill. Vultures wait to scavenge.

The Hunt

Lions hunt at all times of the day, but nocturnal hunts are generally more successful, especially in areas of sparse cover. While the degree of hunting cooperation among lions was a subject of controversy for many years, it has now been accepted that strong and conscious cooperation often occurs. Researchers have witnessed individuals spreading themselves out to flank prey, with some lions moving in to ambush their potential victims. They've also observed lionesses approaching the prey and frequently looking back at the other members of the group to note their position and progress. To date there is no evidence that lions purposefully approach prey from downwind more often than from upwind, though the former strategy is three times as successful. It appears that some leopards may have learned the advantages of hunting from downwind, however.

Lions take a wide variety of prey, depending upon season, situation, and geographic location. In South Africa's magnificent Kruger National Park, which is home to huge herds of impala, these smallish antelope have been found to furnish about half of the lion's food. In most areas about five species usually provide most of a lion's food, with zebras and wildebeest always figuring prominently if available. In Tanzania's Serengeti National Park, lions also prey heavily on buffalo and topi; in Kafue National Park in western Zambia also on buffalo, hartebeests, and warthogs; and in Nairobi National Park, which lies just out of Nairobi, also on hartebeests. Lions sometimes take very large animals such as elephant calves or young rhinos, as well as adult buffalo. Generally prey between two hundred and 660 pounds (90–297kg) is preferred. Larger prey is more difficult to bring down, and smaller prey does not provide enough meat. Lions will readily scavenge, robbing leopards, cheetahs, wild dogs, and hyenas of prey they have killed.

Lions generally kill smaller animals by slapping them or clutching them with paws, then biting, most frequently on the back of the neck or the throat. Medium-sized prey is pulled down by raking a forepaw over the rump, knocking the animal over. It is then held by the throat, puncturing thin-skinned prey deeply, but strangling thicker-skinned prey without ever breaking the skin. A lion may place its mouth over a victim's muzzle to suffocate the animal.

Very large animals may be hamstrung before being successfully pulled down. In some areas, a surprisingly large number of adult buffalo have had their tails broken off at the root. Some prides learn to take even adult bulls weighing fifteen to eighteen hundred pounds (675–810kg), with one large lion (often a big male) catching the bull's tail in its mouth and rearing back to "anchor" the larger animal while other lions rush in to bowl it off its feet. Sometimes the tail simply snaps off. In South Africa's Kruger National Park, several prides of lions have become adept at taking adult giraffe, which is no easy feat when you consider that this is the fifth or sixth largest land animal, with a big bull stretching twenty feet (6m) in height and weighing over three thousand pounds (1,350kg).

I have been lucky enough to see this situation twice. In one instance in Kruger, several subadult lionesses waited in ambush at a waterhole during dry season. It took hours for the drama to unfold as several adult giraffe gradually worked their way in toward the water, all the while testing the lions. The lions made several abortive, hesitant charges at the huge animals, but did not press these attacks home. The giraffe apparently eventually decided they could handle the situation and, after six hours, finally came on in and slaked their thirst while the chagrined lions watched them.

In another instance a much larger pride of obviously trained animals stampeded three giraffes and chevied them along for over a mile until one of the long-legged brutes stumbled in the fading light and the lions quickly swarmed the off-balance animal to take it down. Once the giraffe was off its feet, it was all over. The lions had learned not to try to strike the huge animals down themselves but to try to stampede them into a vulnerable stumble. Sadly, it was too late for any photos, but I was there at false dawn the next day, all ready to photograph more pride interaction on the huge kill when I discovered that somehow they managed to drag the well-over-a-ton animal back some fifty yards (45m), not only into but *through* very thick cover. I would not have thought it possible if I had not seen it myself. ∎

Left: Here a big male tolerates a small cub feeding literally under his nose. Amazing but not uncommon conduct from such a fiercely lethal animal!
Above: The lion pride, unique among all the cats.

"Man-Eating" Lions

No carnage by an individual lion has ever approached the totals amassed by the notorious tigress known as the "Champawat man-eater," who killed an incredible 438 people in eight years in Nepal and the Kumaon district of northern India before being killed by Jim Corbett in 1911. Nor has any single lion come close to the equally infamous Indian leopard known as the "man-eater of Panar," which accounted for about four hundred victims before Corbett shot it in 1910. Jaguars have been known to kill a limited number of people in South America.

The most famous human-eating lions of all time were the "man-eaters of Tsavo," which preyed on emigrant Indian rail-workers who were building the Mombasa to Kampala Railroad in 1898. These episodes occurred while the crews were putting the rails and bridge over the Tsavo River in Kenya, East Africa, and the lions killed forty people. When finally killed by J. H. Patterson, the engineer in charge of that section of the railroad (he wrote the classic book *The Maneaters of Tsavo*), these lions showed no weakness nor disability, being in fine shape. Man-eating lions prefer to do their killing in prides rather than alone, and the most notable case of man-eating lions took place in southern Tanzania over a period of fifteen years. For no obvious reasons, a family of lions began to kill and eat people around Nombe in the early 1930s. Although the game department immediately organized search patrols, these were unsuccessful, and, little by little, the lions became more aggressive and very astute at avoiding detection.

They killed ninety-six natives in 1941, sixty-seven in 1942, and another eighty-six a year later. After fifteen years of intensive effort, favorable conditions finally resulted in the killing of all fifteen lions, now into the second generation of the murderous dynasty, in 1947. It is estimated that between one thousand and 1,500 people were killed during the fifteen-year period. Again, all fifteen of these human-eaters, male and female alike, were found to be in good condition and fully capable of feeding themselves on the abundant wild game in the area. In another instance seventeen lions killed 128 people in the Ankole district of Uganda.

Single lions have also killed people. A rogue lion in Malawi killed fourteen people in the space of a month while another human-eater killed in Mozambique was responsible for the deaths of twenty-two natives in eight weeks in 1938. There is also a reliable record of a lion killing forty people in what is now northern Zimbabwe before it was shot in 1943. Infirm lions were involved in a number of these cases of single lions turning to human-eating. ∎

Above: Lions are very active in the cool of early morning. Facing page top: A big male rampant in the sub-desert of Namibia's Etosha Park.

The Lion's Subspecies

The variation among lions in pelage color, size, color of manes, and shape of skulls has resulted in extensive taxonomic confusion at the subspecies level. Among living forms, there is only one *species* of lion, *Panthera leo*, named in 1758 by Linnaeus, but zoologists have disagreed about how many valid subspecies of lion exist. Taxonomic thought on lions, as with many other animals, has ebbed and flowed as first the "splitters," those who tended to define more and more separate subspecies, and then the "lumpers," those who tended to recombine the subspecies, have been in scientific ascendancy.

Reay Smithers of the University of Pretoria proposed twenty-four subspecies for the African lion, while other researchers have cited five more for the Asiatic lion. Several of the African races were named on the basis of captive specimens, and are now not well regarded because of the known morphological differences caused by captivity. Many of the remaining subspecies were named on the basis of one or a very few specimens using features such as mane size and color to characterize new subspecies. Subsequent observation has noted such great individual variations within most populations that these previously recognized forms are no longer considered discrete enough to be called a subspecies. Most current consideration recognizes a single African subspecies, *Panthera leo leo*, and a single subspecies for the Asian (Indian) lion, *Panthera leo persica*. Advanced genetic testing techniques have indicated valid differences between these two races.

However, some authorities still question the validity of according the Asian lion separate subspecific status. General thought calls for the Asian lion to be a bit shorter, stockier, and more short-legged than its African cousins with the Asiatic lion also carrying a heavier coat and scantier mane. As long ago as forty years, noted Indian naturalist E. P. Gee suggested that these marginal differences might not be valid since the then extremely small population of Asian lions (perhaps one hundred animals or fewer at that time) was the result of intensive and highly unnatural selection for more than a century, during which the English and the maharajah class systematically removed most of the larger, better-maned males. ■

The Range of the Lion
(*Panthera leo*)

Pride Behavior and Patterns

The lion's sociable way of living is its most distinctive habit. It is the only felid that lives in well-defined, relatively large groups. The lion's habitat preference for relatively open country, its cooperative hunting methods, its prey choice, its communal manner of rearing cubs, and even the development of that remarkable mane are all directly related to its social habits.

A pride is generally defined as a group of resident lionesses and their cubs with attending males, all of which share an area and interact relatively peaceably among themselves. The core of the pride are the lionesses, who are directly related to each other, often siblings, and form a constant group closed to strange lionesses. As female offspring mature, they usually become a part of this closed society. Several factors help to prevent inbreeding. Males born to pride lionesses almost always leave that pride by the time they are sexually mature, usually driven out by the pride's adult males. Also, pride lionesses may mate with males from neighboring prides or nomadic lions.

Adult males are only temporarily with any given pride; it is the adult females that form the stable core. Males may remain with a pride anywhere from a few months to several years and may leave on their own or be driven out by males who then join the pride. When this happens, the first thing the new males do is kill all the existing cubs. Because the lionesses no longer nourish and nurture cubs, they come into estrus and mating commences, this time with the new males. The newly added males are often related to each other, frequently brothers or pride mates of the same age, and they have generally been together as nomads before joining the pride. The number of males per pride varies according to lion density in an area.

In an area of high lion density such as Tanzania's Serengeti National Park, a male needs at least one other male to help defend the pride and maintain pride integrity. In areas of lower density, one male can maintain a pride or one male may associate himself with several prides, as they do in Nairobi National Park. The average size of a pride in Serengeti is fifteen animals, though prides as large as thirty-seven and as small as four have been recorded.

The adult sex ratio in prides is at least two to one, with more females than males. This is not as out of balance as it may appear when you consider that males eat more food yet bring in little food. Females are more agile and are swifter, more efficient hunters than the far larger males. Thus, the disparity in weights between the two sexes means that the pride may have an almost equal weight—as opposed to numbers—of males and females. Though the birth rate is about equal, males suffer a higher mortality when they leave the

pride as young, unseasoned adults that must hunt and provide for themselves even though they are much less proficient than more experienced animals. Thus the *how* of pride formation is the tendency of lionesses to stay with familiar lionesses and defend their territory from strange lionesses, reinforced by males who tend to join the pride and then proceed to drive away strange males.

The *why* of pride formation stems from several major advantages afforded by group living and cooperative behavior. Groups of lions are twice as successful at catching prey than are single lions, and groups are more than twice as successful at taking larger prey. The pride usually eats all of a kill, thereby eliminating the energy drain of guarding the kill. If a kill is not entirely eaten in the first sitting, a pride can successfully guard it while groups of hyenas might well drive away a single lion. Also, although a single lioness will give birth to as many cubs as a pride lioness, twice as many pride cubs will survive due to the advantages of cooperative rearing. ■

Rearing Cubs

Cubs remain dependent upon the pride for two and one-half years, a longer period of dependency than any other cat's. This is necessary because of the longer time needed to teach the cub group hunting skills and, perhaps, to achieve the more complex socialization. Lionesses gain

several advantages from permitting males to associate with the pride. Males are much more active than females in patrolling, scent-marking, and roaring (lions are the most vocal of the big cats, by far), all of which establishes and maintains the pride's territorial claim. Males may guard cubs while the lionesses hunt, and they may even drive females away from a kill so that the cubs can eat. Although males will eat their fill before allowing females to eat, they often allow cubs to eat first.

Generally, resident lions do not harm cubs, though nomadic males or males from neighboring prides will frequently kill them. Prides with a full complement of males are much more successful at raising cubs. George Schaller found in his classic study *The Serengeti Lion* that one pride which lost its males had only a 19 percent cub survival while a comparable neighboring pride with vigorous males had a 46 percent cub survival. Schaller also found that, despite members of both sexes belonging to the pride, males and females tended to associate with adult members of their own gender.

By the time they are thirteen to fifteen months old, lion cubs are about the same size as an adult leopard, weighing about a hundred pounds (45kg). Males undergo a six-month period of rapid growth at three and one-half years, during which they reach adult size and weight and the mane develops to a much greater extent. Females have their first litter at three and one-half to four years. Lions generally live ten to twelve years in the wild, though captive specimens have exceeded twenty years. I personally know of one captive male lion still alive at the ripe old age of 29.

It is one of nature's many astonishing feats that such fierce, lethal animals have evolved a relatively complex and social survival strategy.■

Right inset: A young lion cub goes exploring. Above: The lion's habitat requirements are in some ways directly related to the social structure of the pride. They have survived in all sorts of habitats except the starkest deserts and the thickest forests. They survive in southwestern Africa's Kalahari Desert, where water may be available to them only a few brief periods a year or sometimes not for a whole year, largely by eating tsama melons, which contain large amounts of water, and by efficient use of fluids from their kills.

However, they do not survive in the densest of forests, due to the very limited number of large herbivores upon which lion prey and the difficulty of keeping a pride together in such low-visibility conditions. Tigers survive in such areas by their more solitary habits and by frequently taking smaller prey, while lions are better suited to group hunting of larger prey. Generally, solitary cats inhabit closed environments.

Overleaf: An adult male pursues a female. Breeding among such lethal animals is extremely complex: If the male is not animated enough, the lioness will often either tease him into excitement or not reciprocte herself. But, if he is too excited, she'll reject him and may even flee for her life.

Physical Characteristics
Size and Weight

For all its glory, the modern lion is the second largest of the cats, after the tiger. It is, however, an impressive animal by any standard. Typical weights for an adult male range from 330 to 420 pounds (149–189kg) and a female from 260 to 350 pounds (117–158kg). Males average eight to nine and one-half feet (12.4–2.8m) in total length (correctly measured "between the pegs" and not "over the curve" and including the tail) with a probable maximum of ten feet, eight inches (3.2m), while a female stretches seven feet, nine inches to eight feet, nine inches (2.3–2.6m) on average. The two longest accurately measured wild lions were both ten feet, eleven inches (3.3m)—monsters shot in the late 1960s in Uganda and in Sudan respectively. These must be regarded as a bit freakish because the lion is, on average, a shorter animal than the tiger. Other measurements in excess of eleven feet (3.3m) have been reported, but these, along with some tigers in excess of twelve feet (3.6m) and thirteen feet (3.9m), are from old skins that have been stretched.

Unlike the tiger, very few lions exceed five hundred pounds (225kg) in the wild. A very large 506-pound, nine-foot, four-inch (228kg, 2.8m) lion was killed in Kenya in 1938, while another one killed in the same country in 1928 weighed 516 pounds (232kg) and measured nine feet, ten and one-half inches (2.96m). A still larger 553-pound (249kg) lion was shot near Kruger National Park in South Africa in 1950; a 585-pound, nine-foot, five-inch (263kg, 2.83m) behemoth was killed elsewhere in South Africa in 1865, and an even bigger lion, slightly under six hundred pounds (270kg) measuring nine feet, eleven inches (2.98m) was shot in the same country in 1912. The heaviest wild lion ever recorded was a mammoth 690-pound (311kg) known "man-eater" shot in 1936 also in the area immediately adjacent to Kruger Park. This weight was so extreme that it was checked several times on local railway scales before being officially accepted.

The Asiatic (or Indian) lion is approximately the same size as its African cousin though perhaps a bit shorter and stockier in build. A male eight feet, nine and one-half inches (2.6m) long and weighing 490 pounds (221kg), *excluding entrails*, was shot in 1884. In about 1620 Emperor Jehangir of India reportedly speared a very large lion in the western part of that country; it measured ten feet, three inches (3.1m) in length and weighed 680 pounds (306kg). ■

Pelage

The distinctive mane is usually present in all adult males, though it can vary greatly in development by area, by individual, and by age. Color varies from ginger to black. The normal coat color is a tawny yellow, which blends in quite well with the dry grasses of the African plain.

In contrast to jaguars and leopards, melanistic (black) lions are very rare. Albino lions have been identified. And, in the Timbavati corridor, which stretches through the approximate middle belt of South Africa's Kruger National Park, a white mutant, which is distinguished from the true albino by having a normal yellow-colored eye, is known. When I was last in this fairly constricted area in late 1990 there was, interestingly enough, not only at least one white lion roaming the area, but also a white kudu, white nyala, and white giraffe, though I did not see any of the latter. The impressive scientific staff at the Kruger park includes such world-class wildlife scientists as M. G. L. Mills and Anthony Hall-Martin, among others. Though I interviewed these people in depth, no one had a clue as to why there was such a unique diversity of assorted white animals in this one smallish area (approximately fifty miles by thirty miles, 80 by 48km), nor whether there was any sort of cause-and-effect relationship involved with that particular area or if it was just a phenomenal coincidence.

In the wild, the now-extinct Barbary lion from North Africa and the Cape lion from southernmost Africa both had the fullest manes and belly fringes of all the lion races. In captivity, the lion's pelage generally darkens and the mane increases in length and thickness and extends further down the back and belly as compared with wild lions. Also, as with other captive big cats, there is considerable difference in skull shape when comparing wild cats to captive animals due to the much greater use of the neck and jaw muscles by wild lions to kill and dismember large prey.

There do seem to be areas where more dark-maned lions occur (such as East Africa's Serengeti National Park and Masai Mara Game Reserve) and areas where manes tend to be thinner (such as in thick, brushy habitats) than the average. However, no one has ever been able to ascribe mane color or conformation as a determining characteristic of separating one lion subspecies from another. This continues to be studied. ■

Left: *Play for these lion cubs, as for all youngsters, not only strengthens them, but also teaches them their capabilities and limitations.* Above: *An extremely rare "white" lion from South Africa.*

LEOPARD: THE SUPER CAT?

ON A BRISK DAWN IN THE SPRING OF 1991, I DOWNSHIFTED AND BEGAN MUSHING MY WAY ACROSS the sandy South African riverbed that coursed through the Mala Mala private game reserve on the western edge of Kruger National Park. Suddenly, to my right on the far bank, I caught a flicker of motion. Through my binoculars I could pick out a fine, prime leopard pulling and hauling an impala ram through the small riverine forest lining the watercourse. Muscles rippled and played down the length of the powerful body as the lithe cat struggled with its burden through the eddying fog. A fine leopard of perhaps 125 pounds (56kg), most certainly a male, was dragging along an adult impala weighing somewhat more than he did. He reached the base of a big fever tree, paused briefly to set himself, and then scrambled straight up the nearly vertical trunk carrying his heavy burden tightly clenched by the throat. ■ Up, up he scrambled, struggling mightily but never pausing, never faltering, until he reached the tree crotch he sought some fifty feet (15m) above the ground. There he stopped to drape his kill safely in the tree's fork, caching it far above any marauding lions that might seek to rob him. Though he was mostly hidden from me, I could tell he was heaving tremendously from the strain. It was an unbelievable show of strength and power. ■ As I sat there and reflected on what I had seen, it brought to mind a similar, yet different, incident I had witnessed in 1986 in Zimbabwe. This time, the leopard was a svelte female of barely seventy pounds (32kg) who had chased a panicky juvenile baboon

A leopard (Panthera pardus) exhibits the steely gaze of this most unpredictable of cats.

a hundred feet (30m) up a slim, bare tree that was—unfortunately for the baboon—isolated from any nearby trees. The cat skittered around and around the crown of the tree pursuing the baboon to the very tips of small branches that would hardly seem able to hold a squirrel. Those limber rods bent and waved frantically under their constantly shifting burdens as she pursued him with a relentless agility and dexterity that had to be seen to be believed.

Finally she cornered him far out on a limb—too far as it turned out, since he lost his footing and fell all the way to the hard, rocky ground far below. The leopardess barely saved herself from a like fall, and then flashed *down* the vertical trunk, which signaled to me that she was truly an arboreal animal of the first order.

The now groggy primate scampered off into a rocky area out of view, where the leopard apparently cornered and killed him. I caught up with her some distance away as she carried her smallish kill up a big tree to feed at her leisure. This chase through the treetops was an exercise in daredevil agility that was fully as impressive as the singular feat of brute strength that I was to see later in South Africa.

THE LEOPARD'S RANGE

Though far from being the largest of the big cats, the leopard (*Panthera pardus*) provokes so many superlatives that some people have called it the "Super Cat." Leopards have the widest east-west distribution of any big cat: Their range stretches from West Africa to the east coast of Africa—more or less throughout that giant continent except for North Africa and a few other isolated pockets (although the population densities do vary tremendously

throughout this huge African range). From Africa, they range east through the southern part of the Arabian Peninsula north into the southern portion of Turkey and farther east through India and Nepal, down through southeastern Asia as far as Java, also arcing north as far as northern China, North Korea, and southeastern Siberia. Interestingly enough, though leopards are still found in limited numbers on the densely populated Indonesian island of Java, they are not now found on the much larger, less densely populated island of Sumatra, lying directly west of Java, even though they must at one time have used this as a bridge to get to Java.

As attested by its huge geographic range, the leopard is one of the most adaptable of the cats and can exist anywhere that it can find enough food and cover. It lives in all types of forests, woodlands, savannas, semideserts, swamps, and rugged mountains. Leopards from mountainous areas are larger than lowland varieties, and desert races and forest leopards are the smallest of all. Leopards are among the most opportunistic of feeders within the highly opportunistic tribe of big cats, feeding on a wide range of prey, including rodents, reptiles, amphibians, large birds, fish if the opportunity arises, and hoofed animals up to twice their own size. Leopards also stalk and kill other carnivores. When leopards stalk other carnivores, they do so with a deadpan facial cast that tells us they are committed to the pursuit of *prey*. This attitude sets them apart from other big cats such as lions and tigers, who also readily kill and eat other carnivores but who display more facial animation thus seeming to treat those animals more as a disruption or as competition than as typical prey.

Above and facing page: Leopards will stalk and kill baboons if possible. A group of angry male baboons or even a single large male can be a formidable adversary especially for a small cat. However, a single sub-adult is no problem at all as we see here.

Where it is persecuted by humans, the leopard is the shyest, most elusive, and most nocturnal of all the big cats. It is commonplace for leopards to be discovered on the very edges of substantial human settlements, including major cities such as Nairobi, so secretive are they, and so adaptable in their diets and lifestyles.

SUCCEEDING AT SURVIVAL

Perhaps the ultimate justification for calling the leopard a "Super Cat" is its success as a species. That is, after all, nature's ultimate accolade. Not only does the leopard have the widest geographic range and widest habitat tolerance of any of the big cats, its numbers in the wild undoubtedly exceed the combined total of all the other seven cats covered in this book.

Although practical methods to directly count leopards on a large scale are lacking, a number of different estimates have been made using a variety of approaches. These figures are broad at best and are usually the basis of much argument among the experts themselves. One of the few points that practically all authorities agree on is that, almost invariably, leopard populations have been shown to have been underestimated when more data became available later.

In 1981, leopard populations in Kenya were estimated by P. H. Hamilton at ten thousand to twelve thousand, "with probably fewer in Uganda and more in Tanzania." In 1985, Zimbabwe's leopards were estimated to number thirty-five thousand. However, researchers Christopher Stuart and Vivian Wilson estimated a far smaller population, saying that in 1988 the combined leopard population of South Africa, Zimbabwe, and Namibia would "probably number fewer than 12,000." Considerable leopard populations exist in other African countries as well.

In 1988, Rowan B. Martin and Tom deMeulenaer published their fascinating and tremendously controversial "Study of the Status of the Leopard in Sub-Saharan Africa." These men developed a complex computer model based primarily on rainfall and, thus, estimated prey densities. Their estimate for the total leopard population of sub-Saharan Africa was "approximately 700,000 animals, with confidence limits of 600,000–900,000." It is interesting to note that the estimate for Kenya derived from this model (10,207 with a lower limit of 5,614 and an upper limit of 18,679) agrees very closely with the most detailed independent estimate ever made for leopard for any country, P. H. Hamilton's 1981 estimate of ten to twelve thousand for Kenya.

It should be stated that fifteen different leading leopard specialists, all members of the Cat Specialist Committee of the International Union for the Conservation of Nature's Species Survival Commission (IUCN/SSP), plus other experts in the field, reviewed Martin and deMeulenaer's study, and they unanimously reject the findings of this model and many of the assumptions made in its construction as well as many of the conclusions drawn from its results. Many have stated that the total leopard population for this enormous region may only be half that indicated by the model, or 300,000 to 350,000. Still, this is a huge number of big cats, far more than all the others mentioned in this book put together, and still does not include the (admittedly far smaller) Asian and Near Eastern populations of the animal.

In any event, the methodology developed for this model and

Leopard: Supreme Stalker?

The leopard is regarded as the best stalker of all the big cats. In one study in the Kalahari Desert in South Africa, researchers followed over 1,300 miles (2,080km) of leopard tracks. Four of the seventeen kills discovered along the way involved extremely long stalks, ranging from nine hundred to 3,700 yards (810–3,330m). The mean distance for the total of 117 stalks was 210 yards (189m). However, due to the openness of this desert and to the extreme wariness of the prey that live there, this distance is undoubtedly considerably longer than the average stalk throughout the leopard's world range.

Interestingly enough, in the majority of cases in this particular study, leopards appeared to know to move from an upwind position (where the game could smell them) to a downwind position (where the game generally could not smell them). This tactic, of stalking into the wind, increased the leopard's hunting success in the observed instances. However, there has been no evidence to indicate that lions have learned the advantage of upwind stalking. A contributing factor might well be that lions appear to take a higher percentage of prey from ambush (at waterholes) and

thus may have to "take it as it comes." Further study is needed in additional locales and differing environments. But it would be fascinating indeed if it could be demonstrated conclusively that a significant number of leopards had definitely learned about upwind stalking success. ■

---

resultant broad, albeit controversial, discussion sparked by it have, on the whole, been beneficial. These computer model estimates for several of the largest leopard populations in Africa are similarly interesting, again remembering that they are strongly disputed by many authorities.

Rank	Country	Predicted Population	Lower Limit	Upper Limit
1	Zaire	226,192	122,144	418,455
2	Angola	62,486	34,367	114,349
3	Zambia	46,369	25,503	84,855
4	Cameroon	41,896	22,624	77,089
5	Central Africa Republic	41,546	22,435	76,445
6	Tanzania	39,343	21,639	71,604
7	Gabon	38,643	20,770	71,541
8	Mozambique	37,542	20,648	68,326
9	Congo	32,394	17,493	59,929
10	South Africa	23,472	12,910	42,954

It is interesting to compare the preceding estimates with

physically gathered, on-ground estimates performed in selected countries throughout the last thirty years or so. As with all population estimates of free-ranging cats, there is considerable conjecture in these figures, also. However, they do generally take into account (sometimes indirectly) several factors such as poaching, political stability, etc., which were not considered in Martin and deMeulenaer's model.

Randall Eaton, in his comprehensive 1977 study, estimated there to be at least 17,300 leopards in the south-central African country of Angola, perhaps as many as 43,300, and that the status was satisfactory—the population did not appear to be declining precipitously. Again, in 1977, Eaton felt there to be at least 13,200, if not 27,500, leopards in the country of Congo, and the status satisfactory and abundant. He also determined there to be at least 13,400 to a high of 26,800 animals in Congo's neighbor to the west, Gabon, and status satisfactory and abundant.

Eaton went on to estimate several southern African leopard populations: The population in Mozambique was estimated at least 16,190 and up to 32,378, and the cat's status was listed as satisfactory; the Namibian population was at least 3,477, if not 6,554, and its status was also termed satisfactory; the South African population was at least 3,800, if not 7,150 (while in 1984, researcher P.

Left: A leopard at ease but beginning to stir will soon set off on the daily hunt. Above: One of the most important reasons for the leopard's success as a species is its ability to protect its kills from competitors.

Among the prey species for the leopard are impala (left), black lechwe (middle), and warthogs (right) illustrating the variety of habitats in which the leopard functions effectively. Facing page: The approach of one of the most perfect engines of destruction ever known—Panthera pardus!

M. Norton theorized the South African population to be 1,500 to 4,000); the Botswana population was at least 3,164, if not 6,646, with the status satisfactory and improving. (In 1988, Christopher Stuart and Vivian Wilson determined that leopards still occur throughout Botswana and distribution has changed little in recent years.)

Eaton also studied East African totals: Tanzanian populations were estimated at 14,740 to 36,100, and the status was satisfactory; Zaire populations were 70,000 to 155,000; Zambia populations were 18,500 to 46,250; Zimbabwe populations were 2,288 to 6,676 (although G. F. T. Child, in 1985, estimated the numbers in Zimbabwe to be as high as 38,000, and Vivian Wilson estimated 10,000).*

WHAT THREATENS THE LEOPARD?

As the most geographically widespread and adaptable of all the big cats, the overall outlook for the species as a whole is comparatively favorable. However, several of the most spectacular and interesting subspecies, whose populations are relatively small, are in great danger of extinction. Though the fur market is still a threat to all leopards, their greatest single threat stems from widespread availability of cheap poisons, which are used by livestock owners who live adjacent to national parks and other places where leopards are protected. Unlike the similarly sized cheetah who often shares the leopard's range, the leopard is a scavenger and thus very vulnerable to poisoning.

The leopard is everything a big cat should be: shy, smart, immensely powerful for his size, effective in both stalking and killing, able to exist in a mind-boggling array of habitats and on a huge variety of prey. It has one of the largest ranges of any large mammal, both geographically and ecologically. Some people have, with the utmost respect intended, jokingly called the leopard the "jackal" of the big cats, due to its ability to exist almost anywhere with the barest habitat left to them.

Long-term outlook for the leopard in the wild, at least for the more common races, is perhaps the best of all among the big cats with the possible exception of that for the puma (due to the general geopolitical stability of the latter's huge North American range). However, the larger, the smaller, and the more spectacular races of the leopard—the very varieties that make the overall species so special, so charismatic—may well precede the tiger into oblivion in the wild. ■

*The author gratefully acknowledges Alan H. Shoemaker's generosity in allowing me to quote extensively from his exhaustive research study, "The Status of the Leopard, *Panthera pardus*, in Nature," from which much of the above data were drawn.

Above left: A leopard cub perhaps eight-weeks-old peacefully begins his journey through a violent life. Above right: A rare "black" or melanistic leopard commonly found in Southeast Asia and less frequently in India and Ethiopia. Facing page: Rolling on or near a kill is generally a sign of satisfaction and contentment—the feline equivalent of pushing away from the table with a sigh after dinner.

The Range of the Leopard (*Panthera pardus*)

Physical Characteristics
Size and Weight

Body length for leopards varies from five to eight and one-half feet (1.5–2.6m); of this length, twenty-eight to thirty-seven inches (70–92.5cm) is tail. Shoulder height can run from eighteen to thirty-two inches (45–80cm), depending upon the sex, subspecies, and geographic location of the animal. Weight ranges from fifty-five to two hundred pounds (25–90kg) with males 50 percent larger than females on average.

Exceptional leopards of two hundred pounds (90kg) of the subspecies *Panthera pardus kotiya* have been recorded on the island of Sri Lanka, where larger predators such as the lion and the tiger have never been present. In the absence of these larger competitors, leopards evolved to occupy a somewhat different niche, and thus they are slightly larger in size, take larger prey, are more social and diurnal, and are less arboreal than other leopard subspecies. Also, a few two-hundred-pound (90kg) leopards have been killed or found high on 17,040-foot (5.12km) Mt. Kenya in central Kenya, where larger body

size is a distinct advantage in the cold climate. Very large leopards also come from Afghanistan, Iran, southwestern parts of what was the Soviet Union, and eastern Turkey.

Though all of the big cats can vary considerably in size, most people are quite surprised to find that the "average" leopard is about the same size as the "average" cheetah or puma. The leopard's justly deserved reputation for strength and ferocity leads most to assume that it is the largest cat of the three.

Pelage

Leopards have relatively elongated bodies set up on short, massive legs. Their tails are relatively longer than the tigers'. The paws are broad and rounded, the ears short. The coat is short and sleek in the tropics and deeply furred in the colder climates. The color of the animals varies greatly from pale straw, tan, or gray-buff to bright red-yellow, greenish (in Zaire), deep yellow, and even chestnut. They have many dark spots, which are small on the head, throat, and chest. On the shoulders, upper arms, back, and flanks, the cat's spots are arranged in rosettes, which usually enclose

an area somewhat darker than the background color. The rosettes can be small or large, thick-rimmed or thin-rimmed, and some have a spot in the center. The throat, chest, belly, and underside of the limbs are white.

In some areas there is a fair amount of melanism in leopards, these black coats being caused by a recessive gene. In a proper crosslight, spots are still clearly visible through the overall black color. Only certain subspecies show melanism, most often in the moist tropical forests of Asia (especially Java) and in the dense forests of Ethiopia. This dark coat color is felt to be an advantage in these dark, forested areas. Strangely enough, there is very little leopard melanism recorded throughout the African rainforest areas—the Congo Basin into Gabon—though these are also dense, dark environments. Often considered the leopard's parallel, the jaguar shows the same proclivity for melanism throughout some of the dense forest regions of its range.

By any yardstick, the leopard is one of the most beautiful animals on earth, and it has paid a dear price to the fur trade for that beauty. ■

Top left: *An idyllic and unusual sight, a mated pair of leopards. This is a mostly solitary, anti-social cat.* Bottom left: *Here an adult leopard skitters up a tree with an agility and power that would put a house cat to shame.* Above: *Though not as agile in the trees as the clouded leopard, the typical leopard is extremely nimble and at home in the trees. It relies on this ability to protect itself and its kills from the far larger lion and tiger which it frequently overlaps in range.* Overleaf: *A leopard prowls a dry streambed in Zimbabwe for bushbuck antelope—a favored hunting ground for a favored prey.*

The Subspecies of Leopard

The leopard is one of the five pantherine cats (along with the lion, tiger, snow leopard, and jaguar), and it is considered to be most closely related to the jaguar because of its similar spotted coat pattern, incidence of melanism, relatively short legs, and powerful, compact body.

Whenever investigating any animal at the subspecies level, especially such a widespread and variable animal as the leopard, it should be noted that taxonomic thought governing validity of the subspecies is constantly changing. Too many people tend to assume (understandably) that if text A says that animal B has X number of subspecies . . . well, that is that. Not so. Some races of leopards were described fifty years ago or longer when scientific thought was much less advanced. Some descriptions of the races were based on as few as one or two individuals, making their status highly questionable. It should also be noted that scientists are human, too. The more races one describes, the more times one's name is in the literature, which may not have been totally lost on some.

At one time or another, well over thirty subspecies of leopard have been described. Today, twenty-seven are often accepted.

Panthera pardus ciscaucsica, described by Satunin in 1914, once inhabited the Caucasus mountain range between the Black and Caspian seas. Many now believe this race to be extinct, as Satunin himself suggested in a letter to an American researcher in the early 1980s. However, the Russian *Red Data Book*, published about the same time, did describe extremely small relict populations as existing as recently as the mid-1980s.

R. I. Pocock also identified another race that is quite possibly now extinct, *Panthera pardus adersi*, as inhabiting the island of Zanzibar off the Tanzanian coast of East Africa. *P. p. adersi* is also not accepted as a valid subspecies by some of today's taxonomists.

The Somali Leopard

Seventeen of the twenty-seven subspecies of leopard are African. For our purposes it is not worthwhile to consider them separately, except to note that *Panthera pardus nanopardus*

of Somalia and the Ethiopian province of Eritrea is the smallest of all the races of leopard; females average only fifty to sixty pounds (23–27kg) in weight, sometimes weighing even less, and males are usually 50 percent larger. This cat was also the most highly prized for fur among all the races of *Panthera pardus*, and for many years a "Somali leopard" fur coat was exceeded in price on world fur markets only by the best Russian sable coats. How sad that this smallest (and *not* highly populous) of the leopards would be the most sought after for the commercial fur trade, to the point of near-extinction.

Leopards in Israel and Turkey

There are other subspecies that carry enough interest of one sort or another to be considered separately. Israel is a particularly interesting area because, though small, it has a relatively rich abundance of fauna because of its location at the crossroads of three continents and also because of the large variety of habitats and climates. The lion existed there until the time of the Crusaders, and the cheetah was last seen in southern Israel in 1959. Three subspecies of leopard were found here or in neighboring areas. *Panthera pardus jarvisi*, first described by R. I. Pocock in 1932, existed in the extremely overgrazed, overbrowsed, and overhunted Sinai Peninsula where very little wildlife now remains. In recent times, the leopards had to prey on the goats of the Bedouin and were, therefore, relentlessly persecuted. Tracks of at least one leopard were seen in 1956, but since 1967 no tracks have been found, and this animal is considered extinct.

The Anatolian leopard (*Panthera pardus tulliana*) of Turkey, Syria, and northern Lebanon is one of the largest—maybe *the* largest—of all the leopard subspecies and is almost extinct. Heinrich Mendelssohn, in a 1990 issue of *Cat News*, stated that this cat was still relatively common in Galilee in northern Israel in the 1920s and '30s, but the last specimen, a very old male, was killed in 1965 before nature conservation became effective in Israel. Anatolian leopards may still survive in Turkey, but local biologists estimate that the population is probably too small

to breed. A leopard was shot near Beypazari, west of Ankara, as recently as 1989. A Turkish biologist, Tansu Gurpinar, is quoted as saying that ten leopards live in the Black Sea's west coastal mountains in northern Turkey and the Toros Mountains in the south. A guide named Vedat Palendoken stated that there are eight to ten leopard sightings each year near Hakkari, near the border with Iraq. However, this area, also known as Turkish Kurdistan, has been closed to visitors for many years and little is known about it. It is obvious that even under the most optimistic of assumptions, this very distinctive subspecies is on the brink of extinction.

Arabian Leopard

Second smallest in size after the Somali leopard, the Arabian leopard (*Panthera pardus nimr*) is one of the smallest of all the subspecies, and it still exists in Israel. A total of perhaps fifteen to twenty Arabian leopards still survive in a very inbred population saved at the brink of extinction in the Judean desert and the mountainous areas of the Negev Desert. These animals probably also survive in Oman, where five were seen in 1983 in the north, and also in the mountainous regions of the south (Dhofar Province). Numbers are unknown, but the population must be highly endangered. This animal also survived in the more remote mountains of southern Yemen, but Jeremy Usher Smith noted that as of 1987, "extinction was imminent." At present there are no captive specimens of either the Arabian leopard (*P. p. nimr*) or the Anatolian leopard (*P. p. tulliana*).

The Persian and Sri Lanka Leopards

The Persian leopard (*Panthera pardus saxicolor*) has the largest captive population of any of the intensively managed captive populations of rare leopards, with a total world population of 148 in fifty-three zoos as of 1990. However, as with some other captive populations of rare big cats, their genetic base is inadequate since it is limited to only nine founder animals. Little is known about this animal in the wild.

The Sri Lanka leopard (*Panthera pardus kotiya*) is in better condition than some of the other rarer subspecies of leopards, but it is still highly endangered. Charles Santiapillai, a member of the Cat Specialist Committee of the International Union for the Conservation of Nature (IUCN) and Sri Lankan himself, estimated a total wild leopard population of four hundred to six hundred in 1982, and said that areas that were still able to provide suitable leopard habitat were unlikely to support more than six hundred animals. Since then, the Tamil uprising in Sri Lanka has devastated these animals since they were frequently shot and trapped for their hides to finance the armed insurrection. Today, leopard expert Alan Shoemaker estimates there to be only 250. Forested areas declined from 44 percent of the island in 1956 to 25 percent in 1981, and this decline has continued and accelerated since Santiapillai's 1982 estimate. Prospects for long-term survival of this leopard in the wild are bleak at this time. As of 1990, there were forty-nine animals of this subspecies in captivity in seventeen locations throughout the world, and, as Shoemaker noted, they were "in dire need of a larger effective gene pool."

The Javan and Amur Leopards

Biologists note that the Javan leopard (*Panthera pardus melas*) still seems surprisingly common on that crowded island where there is little room for wildlife, but there are no informed estimates as to population size, nor are there any captive populations. This is a small leopard that is black more often than not.

The Amur leopard (*Panthera pardus orientalis*), also called the Manchurian or Korean leopard, comes from the remote areas of the Chinese-Russian border and North Korea and is almost extinct. This particular subspecies is very beautiful and has often been compared with the snow leopard. Living farther north than any of the other typical leopards, and living in harsh conditions similar to the snow leopard's, it too has a long, pale winter coat. The Amur leopard's spot pattern is unlike any other leopard subspecies. The rosettes are widely spaced and of large size with very thick borders, which usually have no spaces or gaps. Amur leopards have unusu-

ally long legs, possibly an adaptation for walking in snow.

The 1980 population in the region of Manchuria in China was estimated to be only thirty to forty animals with the same number predicted for North Korea. Peter Jackson, chairman of the IUCN Cat Specialist Committee, estimated in a 1990 *Cat News* article that "there are no more than about 20 [Amur leopards] in the Soviet far east." Timber interests are removing much of the forests in these areas, which retards the production of mast, a staple for many animals, thus degrading populations of the leopard's favored prey species such as roe deer, wild boar, sika deer, musk deer, and goral. Such authorities as Vladivostok biologists Dimitri Pikunov and Victor Korkishko are attempting a last ditch conservation effort to save this magnificent leopard, but funding in this era of social upheaval is in doubt.

As of 1990, 114 captive Amur leopards lived in twenty-eight institutions worldwide, not including some in China and North Korea. Most of these captive animals were descended from nine founders, which is a limited gene pool to begin with but, worse still, seventy-four have representation from only two founders, one of which is suspected to have had the same genes as the other Amur, in which case there may be only a single founding gene pool. Additional founder stock, either from the wild or from Chinese and North Korean sources, is vital.

The North and South China Leopards

There are two additional leopard subspecies in China, and both create much confusion. The North China leopard, now known as *Panthera pardus japonensis*, has also been known as *Panthera pardus fontanierii* and by other designations. The North China leopard has a large population among the several specifically managed exotic leopard subspecies in captivity, with ninety-four animals in thirty-six institutions in 1990. However, this population is highly inbred.

The situation regarding the South China leopard is very murky. At various times it has been lumped with the Indian Leopard

(*Panthera pardus fusca*) and the Indochinese leopard (*Panthera pardus delacourie*), while other authorities believe it merits a separate subspecies of its own. Whatever the nomenclature or taxonomy, the South China leopard is obviously different in appearance from the North China leopard. Its general color is much more golden yellow, and its fur is much shorter. J. A. Allen of the American Museum of Natural History pointed out that the dorsal hairs obtained from two winter North China leopard pelts were forty millimeters long, versus twenty millimeters for a South China leopard. Interestingly enough, while the Chinese grade South China leopard at one hundred in their fur markets, the North China and Manchurian cats are graded at eighty, and the snow leopard (recognized by most zoologists as "the most beautiful big cat") is only sixty. The Chinese prefer shorter-haired furs. Though leopard coats have never been popular in China, except among Tibetans, leopards were pursued relentlessly for the foreign fur markets. In 1956, eighteen thousand leopards, fourteen thousand of them of the South China variety, were killed. But that was thirty-seven years ago. Nowadays the totals are far lower, and Chinese leopards are extremely rare.

The Indian Leopard

The Indian leopard (*Panthera pardus fusca*), though in no imminent danger of extinction, is greatly reduced in numbers from the turn of the century. In 1989 the total of Indian leopards reported by twenty-three Indian states covering most of the country was 6,767, compared to 4,747 in 1984, according to the official figures released by Project Tiger. However, another very informed estimate places the all-India leopard population at perhaps thirteen thousand to fifteen thousand animals.

Leopards still exist throughout much of their original range in India, but in greatly reduced numbers in many areas and isolated pockets in others. Wherever tiger densities are high, leopard densities are usually low due to competition from the larger cat. However, in many areas where former tiger habitat has been too degraded for the larger cats, it is still good leopard habitat. ■

83

Much remains to be learned about leopards, and all cats in general. Cat literature is incomplete and often contradictory and controversial. But the amount of information available is growing and getting better—even as the subjects disappear forever in the wild.

Commercial, private reserves that attract tourists may be the future for quality game viewing throughout Africa. The Mala Mala game reserve, mentioned in the opening of the chapter, and its neighbors bordering Kruger Park in South Africa have some of the best, most consistent leopard viewing in the world.

Left: Panthera pardus exhibiting the ferocity that has led many to call him the "Super Cat" despite his middleweight status. Top inset: A leopard grooming itself to stay clean. Leopard claws are deeply grooved underneath, collecting matter that may rot and become septic. Thus the leopard's attack, especially in the pre-antibiotic era, was feared above all others. It was almost as deadly as the cobra's! Bottom inset: A male scent-marking his territory to warn other leopards that they trespass at their own risk. This also announces to estrus females that he is here and available.

CHEETAH:
THE SPOTTED WIND

T HE HIGH-HAUNCHED, SPOTTED CAT PADDED ELEGANTLY ACROSS THE DRY PLAIN TOWARD A

bunch of Thomson's gazelles who were nervously twitching their tails. Several of the fleet little antelope moved

toward the cheetah, an apparently irrational yet fairly common gesture that involves the prey actually approaching

the oncoming predator. No one has ever been able to explain this behavior. Without pausing, the cat lowered herself

in a single fluid motion and pressed ahead, looking for all the world like a pedigreed bird dog going on point. I could

not see the cheetah's three small cubs, parked safely by a termite hill in the tall grass of Kenya's fabled Masai Mara.

They were still small and timid enough to hide properly while mom was away. That would change, often fatally, as

they became older and larger. As if on signal, the gazelles exploded away in a cloud of brown dust, with the cat

following on incredible twenty-two-foot (6.6m) bounds. ■ This spectacular run was made possible by the cheetah's

unique spine. The cheetah (*Acinonyx jubatus*) can be compared to another animal we love to watch run, the horse.

Both the horse and the cheetah lift all four feet off the ground during the flexed phase of the bound (when their feet

are crossed underneath the body). But only the cheetah can so fully extend its spine that all four feet are also off the

ground during the maximum extension phase of the bound. This flexion and extension of the back by that remark-

able spine adds about thirty inches (75cm) to the cheetah's total stride so that the cheetah, although a much smaller

A cheetah launches a final explosive attack. The high-impact velocity makes this assault devastating to the small and medium-sized prey that cheetahs specialize in.

animal than the horse, actually has the same maximum length of stride of about twenty-two feet (6.6m).

Furthermore, the cheetah can stride much more quickly than the horse, making more than three strides per second while the horse can barely manage two. Remember: The strides are the same length! Most remarkably, because all four feet are off the ground during two phases of the bound rather than one, the cheetah's feet are off the ground during more than 50 percent of the distance it covers at maximum speed. *The cat is almost flying!*

A cheetah usually begins its chase a full one hundred to 225 yards (90–208m) from the prey, a longer strike distance than any other cat's. For example, a lion seldom begins its chase at more than fifty yards (45m) from the prey. The cheetah's total run is up to 550 yards (495m), again a longer total than any other cat's. The situation I was witnessing was no different. The cat had charged forward when still 150 yards (135m) away from its fleet prey, and it seemed, due to the gazelles' rapid acceleration, that things were hopeless for the cat. Then suddenly, in a blinding flash, the cheetah surged forward in a blur of spots. She reached forty-five miles per hour (72KMH) in only two seconds and continued to accelerate, closing rapidly on the now frantically stampeding antelope.

Barely two seconds later, when she had reached about sixty miles per hour (96KMH), close to her top speed, she was moving almost half again as fast as the line of struggling antelope could manage. She had fixed on a single gazelle, as usual the first one to bolt, and she would not veer from her single-minded quest, even though other animals might be closer or easier to strike. I was witnessing total concentration, with life or death in the balance, and it would all play out in thirty seconds or less.

The skittering antelope target, an adult male, jinked madly to his right in a desperate attempt to turn inside the closing cat and cause it to overshoot and lose ground. The cheetah had anticipated this; she was already slowing to counter such expected turns. Cheetah can follow prey very closely, even at high speeds. Motion and speed researcher Milton Hildebrand has explained that a galloping hoofed animal must lead with its inside foreleg, meaning that the forefoot on the side to which the animal is turning must hit the ground first each time the front feet come down. The cheetah's great advantage is that, due to its more flexible shoulders, it can change direction before the forefeet land, thus turning in midair after zigzagging quarry.

The gazelle desperately cut left in a final attempt to elude the rapidly closing cat. Too late. The cheetah corrected instantly and slapped the smaller animal with a forepaw, leaving a long gash down its side from the wickedly hooked and surprisingly sharp dewclaw, also called the kill-claw, which is part way up the inside of the cat's foreleg. Frequently a cheetah will hook its dewclaw in the victim's side, and by swerving or shifting its own weight backward, literally bowl the prey over. This cat stayed with the wildly tumbling gazelle, and emerged from the huge eruption of dust with her short, rather small canine teeth grasping her prey firmly by the throat in a stranglehold. She continued to grasp its throat for a full twenty minutes, suffocating the gazelle, while her own breath slowed. Experts estimate that, after maximum energy expenditure such as a chase, the cheetah must breathe at 150 to 160 breaths per minute to replenish its oxygen debt. It would take a full twenty minutes of rest for the cat's breathing to return to a normal rate of fifteen to twenty breaths per minute.

During a stupendous athletic feat like this, the rapid expenditure of energy generates heat, pushing the cat's temperature to as high as 105 degrees Fahrenheit (40.6°C)—dangerously close to causing brain damage. Due to her prodigious oxygen debt, this cat rested a full twenty minutes before she rose and padded toward the termite hill where her cubs awaited. She chirped to them, in shrill single notes sounding more like a bird call than anything else, to both reassure them and call them to dinner. The fuzzy, curiously marked cubs straggled out of the grass toward mother.

Southwestern Kenya's fabled Masai Mara Game Reserve extends northward from Serengeti National Park in Tanzania. This lovely stretch of African savanna is grassland interspersed with open acacia woodland, the kind of countryside that is classically "African" and, with its sparkling open vistas, among the most beautiful on earth. Elsewhere, it is possible to view hundreds, sometimes thousands, of large animals at once (such as herds of caribou migrating across the northern tundra) or even to see many different species of large mammals simultaneously (such as chital and sambar deer in India). But only in relatively open areas of Africa such as here in the Serengeti and Masai Mara can one see so many species of large animals simultaneously. Better yet, prey animals are often interacting with one or more large predators. I have had as many as nine species of large mammals in view at once. Words like paradise and Eden come to mind, yet even they fail the task of describing such a scene. Even today, when Africa's natural world is hardly a shadow of what it was a mere generation ago, these Elysian Fields are still balm for the soul. Top: A wildebeest migration. The massed herds of blue wildebeest, upwards of a million animals, trade back and forth between the Serengeti and the Mara, with adults providing prime lion prey while smaller calves providing prey for leopards, wild dogs, and occasionally cheetah. A wildebeest cow will turn to defend her calf from a cheetah, whereas she will not from a lion. Bottom left: Thomson's gazelles, classic cheetah prey. Bottom right: Wild dogs, shown here feeding on Thomson's gazelles, are the only large predator in Africa with a more successful ratio of kills to attacks than the cheetah.

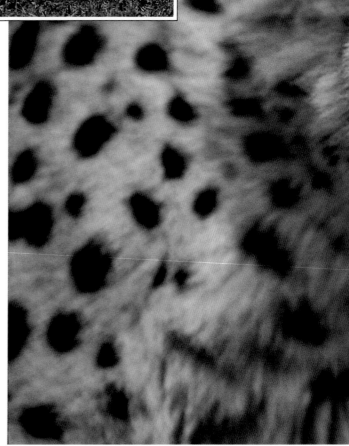

THE OUTLOOK FOR THE CHEETAH

Cheetahs are among the most specialized, atypical, and, in some unique ways, endangered of all the big cats. It is no wonder that so many cat-fanciers become, in short order, cheetah-addicts. These strange cats are beautiful, beguiling and—to some of us—incredibly forlorn and precious. The outlook for cheetahs is mixed but generally negative. Cheetahs favor open lands, which most easily lend themselves to human settlement and cultivation. To make it worse, cheetah have severe genetic problems not experienced by any other wild cat.

Cheetahs are the low man on the predator totem pole and cannot defend their kills or young successfully against most competitive predators. They are basically diurnal sight hunters and thus are more severely impacted by high-density tourism such as that found in East Africa. Because they do not return to feed a second time on kills, they kill relatively more often, making them the sworn enemy of livestock interests.

There are some mildly encouraging factors. The plight of the cheetah has captured the lay public's imagination as that of few other African animals, save perhaps the black rhino and the elephant. Seven to ten years ago, the average American probably could not distinguish cheetah from the other two spotted big cats—leopards and jaguars. That has changed dramatically. Also, a recent study in Kenya, by Patrick Hamilton of the Wildlife Conservation and Management office, suggests that cheetahs can live with humans far better than lions or leopards, and they may benefit from the exclusion of the other two species. Since cheetahs rarely scavenge for food, they are less susceptible to poison. Hamilton also found that many of the cheetahs he studied had adapted like other cats to hunting more at night and to preying on much smaller quarry, such as hares and guineafowl.

Some call the cheetah Pharaoh's leopard, a grand aberration, or the spotted wind. Call it what you will, the cheetah is by any reckoning one of the most distinctive animals on earth consummately engineered and specialized to do one thing and do it supremely well: to run to earth speedy and agile prey.

Cursed by a genetic history of tragic consequence, severely impacted by humanity and its ways, this marvelous cat suffers from its very efficiency at catching and killing. One look at its supple grace, its dainty refinement, steals the heart. One glance at its

sizzling speed as it flashes across the land, more airborne than not, in pursuit of prey captures our admiration and envy equally firmly.

Cheetah: the definition of exquisite, chiseled from living flesh. A felicity of strength and purpose, blended with a delicacy that touches the soul with trembling fingers. Topped by a haughty countenance properly fit for royalty, the *ultima Thule* of speed clothed in spots. Can we live in a world with no place for this animal to live and do what it does so spectacularly well—*run* like the wind? ∎

Facing page: *A cheetah strangles her fresh Thomson's gazelle catch and rests from her mighty labor.* Above: *Note the cheetah's small, almost delicate canine teeth. They are very short for a cat this size, and this is a full adult.*

Resident males, often brothers, control territories, while nomadic and solitary females move through these territories.

Physical Characteristics
Size and Weight

Cheetahs average six to seven feet (1.8–2.1m) in length, including a twenty- to thirty-inch (50–75cm) tail, with a shoulder height of thirty-one inches (77.5cm). Their average weights are one hundred to 120 pounds (45–54kg). Though about the same length as leopards, cheetahs are considerably taller than leopards of the same size due to their long, sinewy legs. Their bodies, although deep-chested, are slimmer than leopards, and their rounded heads are smaller. Cheetahs do not show the size variation that leopards do throughout their range.

Pelage

The coat of the cheetah is coarse, varying from yellowish-gray and tawny to golden or bright reddish-fawn. The markings are small to medium spots, which are not arranged in rosettes as the spots of the other spotted cats—the leopard and jaguar—are. Like other big cats, the adult cheetah's coat pales on the belly and insides of the limbs. On the cheetah's face, a distinctive black line or "tear stripe" extends from the inner corner of each eye to the corner of its mouth, outlining its muzzle. The hard-running, sight-hunting cheetah is the most diurnal of the big cats, and this marking may afford glare protection during some of the bright periods when the cheetah is hunting. It may also break up its facial pattern in tall grass.

In one mutation in coat pattern, the stripes merge into longitudinal lines to form very distinctive and beautiful markings. Discovered in Zimbabwe in 1926 by Major A. L. Cooper, the cats with this mutation are called "king" cheetahs. They were thought for years to be a separate, somewhat larger species named *Acinonyx rex*, but are now known merely to exhibit a color mutation. King cheetahs have been known to live in Zimbabwe, in neighboring areas of northern Botswana, and in northern portions of Transvaal Province, South Africa. They have been seen in the wild only six times, and the only known photograph of one in the wild was taken in South Africa's Kruger National Park in 1974. This is an extremely rare and beautiful cat.

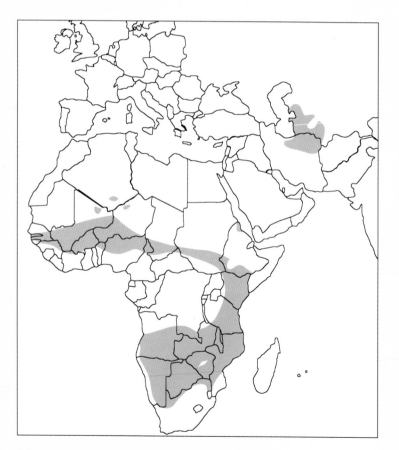

The Range of the Cheetah (*Acinonyx jubatus*)

A cheetah is the hardest working of mothers because she is so vulnerable to other predators and can do so little to protect either her kills or her young.

Both albino and black cheetahs have reportedly been seen, although little specific literature is available about them except for a passage about a white cheetah (*Acinonyx jubatus vanaticus*) being presented to Jahangir, the Mogul emperor of India, in 1608. The emperor said in his memoirs (*Tuzuk-i-Jahangiri*) that "I had never seen a white cheetah. Its spots, which are black, were of a blue color, and the whiteness of the body was also inclined to bluishness." If other white or black cheetahs have existed, they must have been very rare indeed.

Curiously Marked Cubs

It is common for many species to be lighter on their undersides and darker on their backs and flanks, breaking up the animal's outline and making it less conspicuous. Strangely, a newborn cheetah has a very dark underside with a much lighter and very conspicuous mantle of longish silver-gray or white fur covering its upper back and the top of its head. This is an extremely unusual color pattern, and some authorities have proposed a fascinating and convincing speculation as to why young cheetahs are marked in such unusual fashion.

The ratel, or honey badger, is closely related to our own badger and wolverine, and like these other big weasels, it is fierce and aggresive out of all proportion to its size. This extremely powerful small animal is capable of defending itself successfully against far larger predators. The ratel is distinctively marked with a dark underside and a much lighter area down its back. Also, it is three feet (.9m) in length, one foot (30cm) in shoulder height, and twenty-five pounds (11.3kg) in weight—about the size of a cheetah cub.

Some feel that the cheetah cub's unique color scheme is designed to mimic the truculent ratel. This hypothesis is further supported by the fact that ratels are distributed throughout most of Africa, the Middle East, and into India—the historical distribution of the cheetah. Further, ratels are generally common throughout most of this huge area, which increases the effectiveness of the cheetah's presumed mimicry, since other predators have discovered just how unpleasant a ratel can be. Cheetah cubs lose this unusual coloration at about three months, just when their size is noticeably outstripping the ratel's and when their locomotion has improved enough so that they can successfully outrun most predators dangerous to them. ■

Here she comes, a symphony of speed!

The Swiftest of the Cats

The fastest authenticated level bird flight occurred in 1942 in what was then the Soviet Union. A spine-tailed swift (*Chaetura caudacuta*) of Asia was reliably measured at 106.25 miles per hour (170 KMH). Most ichthyologists share the view that the fastest short-distance swimmer in the world is the highly streamlined sailfish (*Istiophorus platypterus*), which is found in all tropical waters. While the maximum velocity of this fish is not known for certain, one sailfish yanked out a hundred yards (90m) of line in three seconds (which translates to 68.18 MPH or 109 KMH) during a series of speed trials carried out with a stopwatch at the Long Key Fishing Camp in the Florida Keys between 1910 and 1925.

In 1948, researchers reported a striking example of the fastest terrestrial animal over a sustained distance: the antelopelike pronghorn (*Antilocapra americana*) of western North America. Four bucks traveled at a clocked speed of thirty-five MPH for four miles (56 KMH for 6.4km), and this was only their cruising speed as they showed no evidence of tiring. In 1939, animal speed researchers recorded another buck pronghorn who "kept abreast of the car at 50 MPH [80 KMH]." They wrote: "He gradually increased his gait, and with a tremendous burst of speed flattened out so that he appeared as lean and low as a greyhound. Then he turned towards us at about a 45-degree angle and disappeared in front of the car, to reappear on our left. He had gained enough to cross our course as the speedometer registered 61 MPH [97.6 KMH]." If the car speedometer was reliable,

then the buck must have been traveling at close to seventy-five MPH (120 KMH)as it crossed in front of the car, although this figure is so extreme that considerable doubt must be cast on the accuracy of the report. Other pronghorn have been reliably reported as traveling forty-two MPH for one mile, and fifty-five MPH for one-half mile (67.2 KMH for 1.6km/88 KMH for .8km). The blackbuck, an antelope living in India, is slightly smaller than the pronghorn and almost as fast.

But the fastest burst-speed animal is without a doubt the cheetah. Cheetahs can regularly attain speeds of sixty MPH (96 KMH) during their initial acceleration. In 1960, Milton Hildebrand of the University of California took films of a cheetah not extending itself, and it was speeding along at fifty-six MPH (90 KMH). Other speeds of up to seventy-one MPH (113 KMH) have been reported, but these are less reliable. It is probably safe to assume that the cheetah can, under optimum conditions and over level ground, achieve maximum short-term speeds of close to seventy MPH (112 KMH). By comparison, the maximum speed of a race horse is about forty-three MPH (68.8 KMH) (although it has considerably more endurance), and the fastest racing greyhounds can reach thirty-seven MPH (59 KMH).

This most specialized of all the thirty-seven species of cats has evolved with almost total focus on speed. Take the architecture of the cheetah's shoulder and rib cage. As with most carnivores, the cheetah's clavicle (collarbone) is greatly reduced in size, its rib cage is flattened on the sides and has relatively greater depth, and it has

narrow, almost vertical scapulas (shoulder blades). All these arrangements serve to increase the effective length of the forelimbs and, therefore, lengthen the cat's overall stride. Of course, the animal with the longer stride goes farther with each stride and thus travels faster for the same rate of stride. Horses, gazelles, and other ungulates have lost their collar bones entirely to further lengthen their strides, but this limits their movement to strictly forward or backward. The cheetah turns with more agility because it retains a small collar bone and thus the ability to pull its feet toward or away from a hypothetical line that would extend in the direction the animal is running. Thus evolution has enabled the cheetah, other things being more or less equal, to out-turn or turn inside of its ungulate prey.

Furthermore, the cheetah's flexible shoulder and spine allow it to do just that—flex—enabling the cheetah to *effectively* increase the length of its front legs. In other words, if you took a tape measure to the foreleg and hind leg bones, you would find that the cheetah's front legs are shorter than its hind legs. But the cheetah's anatomic adaptations serve to increase its foreleg stride to the same length as a hind-leg stride. This allows effortless coordination of fore and hind limbs while trotting or running. Animals with rigid shoulders cannot increase the effective stride-length of their forelegs. The longer hind legs are forced to take shorter strides because they are limited to the stride-length of the shorter forelimbs. If the horse could increase the effective length of stride for its forelegs to match its longer hind legs, its total stride-length would be considerably increased, and thus its speed would be much greater.

The actual length of the limbs, as well as the modified shoulder architecture, also reflects cursorial adaptation in running animals. The longer the limbs, the longer the stride, giving a speed advantage. Compare the longer legs of the cheetah with the short, well-muscled legs of the more arboreal leopard or jaguar. This lengthening is accomplished by extending the more distal leg elements (the parts farthest away from the body). There is also that supremely flexible cheetah spine, which serves to lengthen stride still more. These adaptations are found in all felids, but are more extreme in the cheetah.

Oddly enough, the cheetah does not have *proportionately* longer legs, relative to its body length, when compared to two other big cats. The puma's and snow leopard's hind limbs are equally long and, in other respects, the snow leopard's body proportions are also very similar to the cheetah's. The cheetah's longer-legged appearance compared to these other two is partially due to its more upright stance and its smaller head, and partially due to the slenderness of the limb bones in the cheetah's legs, especially the distal elements. The speed of the cheetah's stride is increased significantly by this lightening of the limb bones, which are much thinner for their length than those of any other felid of comparable size. This thinness of limb also makes the cheetah's relatively high body weight curious and, as yet, inexplicable. ■

Above: *A svelte cheetah* (Acinonyx jubatus) *alertly scans the horizon both for prey and for the ever-present danger to her from larger predators.*
Right: *These very young cheetah cubs cower against their mother for protection. Sadly, she is severely limited in what she can do to protect them from stronger predators.*

Further Adaptations for Speed

Although the cheetah's specialized anatomy is built for speed, it is even more specifically designed for blinding burst-speed. Endurance has been sacrificed toward that end. If cheetahs do not catch their target within five hundred to 550 yards (450–495m), they must quit, while their ungulate prey can run at speed for a couple of miles or more. The ungulate's leg structure helps to extend its endurance by using an arrangement of ligaments that acts as a spring, helping to automatically straighten out the leg after weight has been put on it, thus increasing efficiency. By contrast, the cheetah's leg propulsion has to come entirely from muscular force.

The cheetah's small canine teeth, crowded and rather close to the other teeth, are not efficient for killing large prey quickly with the typical felid cervical or neck bite. Some speculate that these rather small, inefficient teeth result from another modification for speed—enlarged nasal passages, which are necessary for increased air intake. These crowd and restrict the roots of the teeth, making them less lethal. The cheetah takes smaller prey than other cats its size, and it must strangle them by a lengthy chokehold on the throat lasting up to twenty or twenty-five minutes. Although the cheetah's nasal passages, heart, lungs, and adrenals are enlarged, the heavy breathing required for up to thirty minutes after a chase is testament to the enormous energy expenditure. A cheetah's heat build-up from a four-hundred-yard (360m) sprint raises its temperature to an almost lethal 105 degrees Fahrenheit (40.6°C). A strenuous chase much beyond 550 yards (495m) would probably kill it.

A final cursorial adaptation involves the cheetah's paws and claws. There is no webbing between the toes, and the individual digits are separated more than is typical for a felid. All the toe pads are very hard and sharp and are pointed at the front, serving as cleats when the animal is braking or turning at high speed.

There is a lot of confusion regarding the cheetah's claws, and it is often stated that they are nonretractable. This is not true. The cheetah's claws are almost as retractable if not as fully retractable as other felids'. The ligaments necessary for retraction are present and function well. The differences between the cheetah's claws and those of other big cats are that the cheetah's are shorter and straighter (except for the dewclaws), and there are no sheaths of skin covering the retractable claws as is the case with other felids. Thus the retracted claws remain clearly visible on top of each digit, and this is visually misleading. Most of the blunting of the claws is probably due to ground contact resulting from extension during the chase for increased traction.

■

How the Cheetah Hunts

Because of their supple, lightly muscled builds and small teeth, cheetahs are not physically able to defend their kills from larger or stronger predators such as lions, hyenas, wild dogs, or even, in some cases, vultures and jackals. If a lion, hyena, or wild dog is hurt and unable to hunt, there is a good chance it can survive by scavenging off the kills of others. Even the solitary leopard, because of its nocturnal ways and method of hunting by ambush, has a chance to survive if injured. However, the cheetah cannot scavenge and must always be in top form in order to run down and dispatch its fleet prey. This narrows the window of suitable prey species for cheetahs by inhibiting them from taking large prey.

Because they can't defend their kills from others, cheetahs feed only once off a kill and then do not return. For this reason, and because they never attempt to scavenge off the kills of others they must kill far more often than the leopard. This makes them the sworn enemy of game ranchers and cattle raisers in Namibia and in other areas of their range. Fortunately, they are not as vulnerable to poisoned bait, a method used all over the world to eliminate all kinds of predators, since they do not scavenge.

Since they must kill small prey daily, it is fortunate for cheetahs that their success ratio is far higher than other felids'. British biologist Brian Bertram conducted one survey in Serengeti National Park in

Above: *The cheetah accumulates an enormous oxygen-debt in order to achieve such high speeds for short distances.* Above right: *The cheetah will not return to this kill after her initial feeding on it.*

Tanzania in 1979. He showed that the estimated 250 to five hundred cheetahs in the park were successful in 37–70 percent of their chases. By comparison, the eight hundred to 1,200 leopards estimated to be present in the same park were successful only 5 percent of the time. The two thousand to 2,400 lions, though cooperative hunters, were successful only 15–30 percent of the time—less than half as often as cheetahs. The other, still more cooperative hunters that rivaled or surpassed cheetahs in success ratio were the three thousand to 4,500 spotted hyenas, being successful 35 percent of the time, and the 150 to three hundred efficient wild dogs, being successful 50–70 percent of the time. However, the cheetah's extremely high success ratio remains an astonishing accomplishment for a single animal most often hunting without allies.

A relatively small mouth-gape also limits the cheetah's prey size. Presumably a larger gape allows a cat to catch and dispatch animals with a larger neck—in other words, a more "profitable" prey size. Cats tend to kill the largest possible prey animal in order to maximize return on the energy expenditure required for the kill. Therefore, although different-sized cats may kill prey in overlapping ranges of size, each will concentrate on different-sized prey within that range.

Cheetahs prefer relatively small ungulates. On the open savannas of East Africa, this means the Thomson's gazelles, which average forty to fifty pounds (18–23kg), although cheetahs will also take the larger

Grant's gazelle and impala, as well as the far smaller hares. In the woodlands of South Africa's Kruger National Park, they prey primarily on impala (which are a bit more than twice as heavy as the Thomson's gazelles), since impala are far and away the most prevalent animal in that huge park. In the desert areas of Namibia, western South Africa, and Botswana, they primarily concentrate on springbuck, which are seventy to eighty pounds (32–36kg). Springbuck are the only gazelle native to southern Africa. Throughout their once-broad range, cheetah have always shown a marked preference for gazelles, when available, since this group of fleet, small antelope seem almost engineered for the cheetah.

George Schaller has documented two male cheetahs taking a yearling topi, a fleet middle-sized antelope, which weighed about two hundred pounds (90kg). I was present the day after a rare case of a single cheetah killing an adult ostrich weighing up to three hundred pounds (135kg) or more in Namibia's Etosha National Park. Hans Kruuk documented cheetahs preying on mid-sized animals such as wildebeests, yearling kudu, and yearling zebra. Whereas a mother wildebeest will abandon her calf to a lion, she will turn and defend it from a single cheetah. Since cheetahs expend such a tremendous amount of energy during an extended chase, they are simply too exhausted by the time they bowl the prey off its feet to subdue struggling prey of relatively large size. ■

The Subspecies of Cheetah
The African Subspecies

Seven subspecies of cheetah have been recognized, five of them in Africa and two in Asia. They are so similar that there is considerable doubt as to whether subspecific identity is warranted, especially among the African races. Researcher Norman Myers estimated in the early 1970s that there were about fourteen thousand cheetah present in twenty-two countries in Africa and further speculated that there would be fewer than ten thousand by 1980. There is a broad consensus that the cheetah population is declining drastically throughout Africa. A pan-African survey of cheetah begun in 1989 by Tim Caro and Paula Gross should give us a clearer picture of the situation.

The southern African cheetah (*Acinonyx jubatus jubatus*) is the most common, with five hundred cheetahs estimated in South Africa as of 1989 and 470 in Zimbabwe in 1986. As of 1987 Jose Tello estimated that fewer than one hundred cheetahs were left in Mozambique. Ten years ago, more than six thousand cheetahs were estimated to remain in Namibia, their world stronghold. But few live in Namibia's Etosha Park where lions (who tend to crowd out cheetahs) occur in the highest density of any place on earth; in fact, well over 95 percent of Namibia's cheetahs live on unprotected, private lands.

Due to the cheetah's highly efficient ability to kill and its habit of making a fresh kill each time it must eat, it is far more destructive, animal for animal, to stock farmers and game ranchers than are many other predators such as leopards. By 1990, the estimate for Namibia's cheetah population had shrunk by more than half—down to two thousand to three thousand animals—partially due to relentless persecution by these commercial interests. Actually, as with most major conservation issues, the matter is complex and far from being as simplistic as it might appear on the surface. I have had extended discussions with several major game ranchers in Namibia who went to considerable trouble and expense to chase cheetahs with hounds and capture them alive in order to try to dispose of them without fatality.

Several cooperative programs intended to ship these cheetah from Namibia to Kenya in the mid-1980s did not work out, due to political problems. With the changing African political climate, hopefully some of these programs can be reestablished. Some leading conservationists such as Zimbabwe's Vivian Wilson have also suggested that we legalize sport hunting of cheetahs, with severe limits and costs, in those areas where populations might support it, giving a direct economic value to the animals and thus encouraging commercial interests to preserve them. As distasteful as this approach may be to many, it has proven to benefit leopards in certain areas. Needless to say, this is a passionately controversial issue that can cause sparks to fly whenever seriously proposed.

There are two subspecies credited as being in East Africa: *Acinonyx jubatus raineyi* in Kenya, and *Acinonyx jubatus ngoronogorensis* in Tanzania and adjacent Zaire. Brian Bertram esti-

mates total East African cheetah populations to be "fewer than 3,000, and declining." Little information is available on the current status of and population estimates for the other two African subspecies: *A. j. soemmeringii*, which formerly inhabited a huge east-west belt from sub-Saharan Nigeria to Somalia, and *A. j. hecki* of the Mediterranean coastal country of Algeria and the coastal areas of Benin (formerly Dahomey).

The Asian Races

There are perhaps two Asian subspecies, both of which are felt to have more validity than the proposed African forms. They differ from the African forms by having a slightly larger body size, longer fur, and darker coloration. However, some consider the Transcaspian cheetah (*Acinonyx jubatus raddei*) of the Caspian Sea area to be the same as the India and Middle East subspecies (*Acinonyx jubatus venaticus*).

In any event, the cheetah (*Acinonyx jubatus raddei*) is extremely rare, if not already extinct, east of the Caspian Sea in Turkmenistan, which was this cat's final Asian redoubt. A story is related of four sightings of wild cheetahs and one discovery of a skull and piece of skin in Turkmenistan between October 1975 and July 1983 (as told by A. V. Gorbunov in his master's thesis). The last sighting was of a female with her two cubs. Still, if there are any cheetahs still surviving in the wild in this area, it is highly doubtful that they will be able to sustain themselves. Currently there is heated debate in some quarters as to whether African cheetah should be introduced to this area to augment any remaining wild stocks and fill the habitat. Some feel this would mongrelize the genetic stock of any possible remaining Asian cheetah and should be avoided at all costs. Others feel that there is no significant difference genetically and that, for all practical purposes, the native cat is already gone.

Acinonyx jubatus venaticus once ranged widely from southwest Asia to India. It has been reported variously as being extirpated in the wild in India in 1948, 1951, and 1956, and is now felt to exist only in Iran in extremely small and separate populations. During the 1970s, there were reports of 250 cheetahs in Iran, but Dr. Paul Joslin, who was working with the Iranian conservation people at that time, feels this to be an overestimate. Joslin further states that if gazelles were protected in Iran, cheetahs would survive. In 1985 Masood Mowlavi wrote, "The Asiatic cheetah was thought to be on the verge of extinction in Iran about two decades ago but, due to sound conservation practices for this species and its habitat, it has made a remarkable comeback in recent years." Although the exact number of cheetahs is not known, it is believed to be increasing in Iran. Khosh Yeilagn Protected Area in northeastern Iran supports the highest population of Asiatic cheetah in the world, with groups of one to nine having been sighted by various investigators there.

Dr. Kh. Ammarlooi, director of the Natural History Museum in Tehran, also wrote in 1985 that two cheetahs were sighted in the Kavir National Park in Varamin (to the south of Tehran) and that there were several in the Touran Protected Area. He reported only

one captive in Iran, a female in the Mashad Zoo. Paul Joslin,IUCN Cat Specialist Committee member, recorded in 1984 a possible cheetah population of thirty in the Khosh Yeilagn Protected Area in northeastern Iran. The rest of the population was scattered all over with a "reasonable guesstimate" of a hundred-plus in the whole country. However, it must be cautioned that the above was based on information obtained from 1973 to 1976. With the subsequent political turmoil in Iran, the outlook for the cheetah has not been promising. It is felt that some Asiatic cheetahs still survive in the remote region where the international boundaries of Afghanistan, Iran, and Pakistan coincide, with the possibility of a few survivors in adjacent areas of southwestern Asia.

The last Asiatic cheetah in Iraq was reported in 1928. On December 9, 1959, a cheetah was spotted running along the Israeli road fifty miles (80km) north of Eilat at night and what was believed to be the same animal was seen again thirteen days later. The last known wild cheetah in the Sultanate of Oman was shot in Dhofar Province in 1977. The last record from Jordan is of a female and her cub killed in 1962.

No biopsies have ever been carried out on Asiatic cheetahs. In order to determine the degree of difference between Asiatic and African cheetahs, blood and skin samples of the former are being sought by Daniel Krause of NOAHS Center, National Zoological Park, Smithsonian Institution, Washington, DC 20008, USA. ∎

All cats spend a lot of time resting, but the cheetah especially needs it because of the prodigious amount of energy burned during their short but demanding chases after prey.

The Cheetah's Genetic Tragedy

The cheetah has always been difficult to breed in captivity, and when breeding has occurred, survival of young has always been low. In the 1500s the Mogul emperor of India, Akbar, kept over one thousand cheetahs for hunting, but only one litter of three was ever born. Although cheetahs have been exhibited in western zoos for nearly two hundred years, captive breeding did not succeed until 1956 at the Philadelphia Zoo. Breeding success has increased dramatically in the last twenty years, but it is still difficult, and survival rates, compared to those for other captive cats, are still very low.

Part of the problem is that female cheetahs will not come into estrus if kept permanently with a male, and for many years zoos always tried to exhibit pairs of animals. By keeping males and females separate and reintroducing them periodically, females can be stimulated to come into estrus. To some extent, this parallels the situation in the wild, where females are nomadic and solitary, and males are territorial and often live in coalitions.

Researchers eventually discovered signs that indicated both wild and captive cheetah populations suffer from severe inbreeding. In 1985, Stephen O'Brien of the National Cancer Research Institute in Maryland, together with his research partners, looked at captive populations to verify this, and found that although litter size was often large, sperm concentration and level of fertility was low (29 percent viable, versus 71 percent for the domestic cat). Survival of cubs was often less than 40 percent, extremely low for captive situations. Also, cheetah skulls are highly asymmetrical, especially when compared with those of other cats—another indicator of inbreeding. It was found that captive cheetahs are so identical genetically that it is possible to carry out successful skin grafts between any two captive cheetahs, an amazing and very unfortunate fact. In fact, the researchers found that captive cheetah are more inbred than some highly inbred strains of laboratory mice. All of these factors result in low birth rates, low survival rates, and increased vulnerabil-

The "king" cheetah, an extremely rare and unique color morph of the cheetah with no parallels found among leopards or jaguars, the other large spotted cats.

ity to disease.

Even more distressing, the researchers discovered that these problems were not limited to the captive population. Wild cheetahs from South Africa were also virtual genetic clones of each other. Two years after their first study, O'Brien and his colleagues found that cheetahs from East Africa had a genetic diversity of about 4 percent—somewhat better than the South African cheetahs' 2 percent, but still extremely inbred.

The Whipsnade Zoo in England has had more than 150 cheetah births since 1967, and part of this success has been attributed to the crossing of East African and South African cheetahs. The two populations are so inbred that the existence of separate subspecies in

eastern and southern Africa seems highly doubtful. O'Brien and his coworkers concluded that the once-cosmopolitan cheetah suffered a severe population decimation about ten thousand years ago at the end of the last Ice Age and must have been reduced to a total population of ten animals or less. This drastic population crash and subsequent slow recovery is very similar to problems faced by some captive animal populations today, where genetic diversity is quickly lost due to a too-small founder population. During the 1800s, the South African cheetah population suffered an additional population bottleneck, probably due to human persecution. This reduced still further the anemic genetic diversity in South African cats. ■

Raising Cheetahs in Captivity

On May 12, 1981, the forty-seventh litter of cheetah cubs at Ann Van Dyk's De Wildt Cheetah Centre was born. This adjunct of the Pretoria Zoo in South Africa's open farmland is the personal extension of one courageously dedicated woman. Here, more than six hundred cheetahs have been born, about twice as many as at any other facility in the world. This particular litter of five raised De Wildt's cheetah births to 177, and one of the male cubs was the first "king" cheetah ever born in captivity. When I recently visited her, I asked Ms. Van Dyk if the appearance of this beautiful color mutation was a happy accident. She assured me that it was not, and that producing king cheetahs had been one of her driving goals since she started the facility. De Wildt has now produced more than fifteen of these magnificent cats. ■

Top: A "king" cheetah, contrasted with a typical cheetah. Above: Ann Van Dyk and Mike Penrith of the Pretoria Zoo.

Evolution of the Cheetah

Although much of the dating of the evolution of the evolution of the big cats is still speculative, many authorities agree that the ancestral lines of the cheetah diverged about five million years ago (MYA), and the forebearers of the modern cheetah originated one to three MYA. *Acinonyx jubatus* appeared in the Pleistocene Epoch, which began about 1.9 MYA and ended ten thousand years ago. Two cheetahs are known to have lived in North America: *Acinonyx studeri* from 2.5 MYA and *Acinonyx trumani* from as recently as twelve thousand years ago. These Pleistocene cheetahs were superbly adapted to a running lifestyle, and they inhabited grasslands and steppes as do their current counterparts.

The oldest known cheetah fossils come from the giant *Acinonyx cinomonx* of France, and date back to about five MYA. This cat was three times as large as the modern cheetah, about the size of the modern lion, and was less cursorial than its modern counterpart, though it was definitely adapted to run. Following the evolution of most cat species, cheetahs have shown a decrease in body size until the present day, a transformation that most certainly improved their high-speed running ability. ∎

Because it is about the same size as the leopard and often lives alongside it, the cheetah is often compared to the sturdier, more nocturnal spotted cat. What is interesting is that although the two are grossly similar in size and range, they show huge differences in the way they evolved to make a living in the wild. Right: An extended group of cheetahs rests in the warm afternoon sun of Kenya's Masai Mara and waits for the cool of later afternoon to go on the hunt.

JAGUAR:
KING OF THE RAINFOREST

THE WAXY GREEN FOLIAGE IMMEDIATELY IN FRONT OF ME SHIVERED AND DANCED EVER SO slightly. And again, a bit more strongly. The leaves looked like the surface of water, with a fish slightly beneath it delicately mouthing bait before striking. Slowly a massive head, set off by glowing eyes, materialized silently in the shredding morning mist. *El tigre* had come to call. I thought, "No wonder so many of the native peoples attributed mystic or totemic qualities to this great cat through the ages." ■ As the questing head eased further forward, I saw the massive shoulders, set up on ridiculously short, seemingly bowed legs, emerge from the verdant curtain. Even though this adult male jaguar here in Belize weighed only about 125 pounds (56kg), hardly half as much as some of his giant cousins in the more open areas of South America, he was an impressive brute. Blocky, solid, stolid. Beautifully marked with black spots and rosettes throughout his yellowish-brown hide, he was a powerful animal. He was a leopard with a prizefighter's face and a physiognomy run amuck—as if on steroids. ■ I had come to Belize in hopes of seeing a wild jaguar (*Panthera onca*) in the Cockscomb Basin Jaguar Preserve, the world's first and only protected area specifically focused on the jaguar. This pioneering conservation project is the result of an extended study of the jaguar by the New York Zoological Society's Alan Rabinowitz from January 1982 through January 1984. With a jaguar every five square miles (13sq. kg), this is one of the most densely populated jaguar habitats in the world. Sadly, I did not see my wild

A beautifully marked adult jaguar (Panthera onca) forages for food along a lush watercourse in the forest.

jaguar—few people have; the brute I encountered was one of a captive pair in a nearby natural enclosure.

THE JAGUAR AND THE FUR TRADE

Anyone who remembers femmes fatales of the silver screen, from Bette Davis to the incomparable Greta Garbo, dragging a jaguar coat across the floor with a sangfroid no mere male could ever match, understands the hold these furs have had on so many peoples' imaginations through the ages. Nor does the observer have to be a rocket scientist to realize how devastating such a commercially valuable pelt has been to these animals. Local tribespeople have coveted these rich pelts for various totemic and religious reasons back to the dim dawn of prehistory. But it was organized, commercially funded harvesting by "more highly developed" societies for perhaps the last century that has almost been the death knell of this splendid animal (and many of his other spotted-fur felid cousins throughout the world).

In Central and South America in the early 1900s, the jaguar was hunted in large numbers for its skin. We have now found that this overharvest, combined with increasing human destruction of habitat, caused the jaguar's numbers to decline greatly by the 1960s. Because of that, the fur trade then began to shift its attention to the smaller cats.

Fur-wearers in the United States were the major market of Latin American cat skins until the 1970s, although increasing numbers of skins were imported into Europe during the 1960s, especially into what was then the Federal Republic of Germany. Brazil was the major exporter of jaguar skins, although significant numbers were also shipped from Paraguay, Bolivia, Peru, and Colombia. The number of skins taken from jaguars was staggering. In a 1971 report based on official Brazilian statistics, R. W. Doughty and N. Myers revealed that Brazil alone exported over 104,400 pounds (46,980 kg) to various countries—solely in 1969. It is probable that not all legal skins were reported; certainly illegal skins were not. Probably twice as many skins were taken as were reported because hides were often inadequately skinned, stored, or tanned, resulting in having to discard those skins as unsuitable. And unreported in the export ledger was the fact that when females with young were killed, their dependent young died as well.

In a subsequent report, Myers listed the total of cat skins legally entering the United States from all Latin American countries. For jaguars alone, it was a total of 13,516 in 1968; the number was 9,831 in 1969; and in 1970 the total was 7,758. For all spotted cats—which were lumped under the name "ocelot" although actually about seven species were hunted—the totals of skins exported were obscene: 128,966 in 1968; 133,069 in 1969;

Although it is easy to mistakenly correlate CITES Appendix I listings to the U.S. Fish and Wildlife Service's "Endangered Species" list, they are not exactly the same. Appendix I species are regarded as the most endangered species and are the most restricted species as far as international commerce. CITES regulates only international commerce for the listed animals. Therefore, if a country wanted to allow sport hunting and/or commercial harvesting of a cat for use within its own borders, it could do so, even if that animal were protected from international trade by CITES. Above: El tigre stirs in the cool forest morning. Left: A jaguar at rest in the heat of a Belize forest.

The Range of the Jaguar

The jaguar, along with the clouded leopard, is possibly the least-studied big cat in the world. Considering its still-large geographic range and large numbers (relatively, though rapidly decreasing), as well as its long history of interaction with humans, the jaguar is arguably the least-known big cat of all. Like almost all their cat brethren, jaguars are in severe trouble and face an uncertain future at best in the wild. Sparse but sustaining populations of jaguars ranged into Texas, New Mexico, Arizona, and even Southern California well into this century. Unfortunately, fifty years later, the northernmost population is in the southern portions of the Mexican states of Tamaulipas and Sinaloa, about eight hundred miles (1,280km) south of the U.S. border. Concurrently, the southern boundary of the jaguar's range in South America has receded from Argentina's Rio Negro River to the northern part of that country—a full fourteen hundred miles (2,240km).

Researchers Wendell Swank and James Teer estimated that within the United States, Mexico, and Central America the jaguar has lost 67 percent of its range, and within South America it has lost about 38 percent. Established populations of jaguar are judged to be extirpated in the United States, El Salvador, Uruguay, and Chile, and they are facing a similar end in Argentina, Costa Rica, Paraguay, and Panama.

Swank and Teer further described the jaguar's remaining range still occupied north of South America—an area that is 33 percent of the cat's historical range—saying that the jaguar was "greatly reduced" in over 28 percent and "reduced" in over 47 percent. The limited good news is that the "King of the Rainforest" seems to be holding its own or perhaps even increasing over the remaining 25 percent. The Peten department in northern Guatemala and areas surrounding it in southern Mexico and western Belize still have high densities of jaguars.

Swank and Teer also reported that, in the 62 percent of its habitat still occupied in South America, the jaguar is "greatly reduced" in 16 percent and "reduced" in 20 percent. The population is sustaining or even increasing over the remaining 64 percent. The Amazon basin in Brazil, and the areas influenced by the Amazon in southern Venezuela, French Guiana, Surinam and Guyana, eastern Colombia, and Peru and Bolivia have resisted human development and, in turn, provide some sanctuary for the jaguar. ∎

and 87,645 in 1970. And these numbers are in addition to the jaguar skins. Inclusion of the jaguar in Convention on International Trade in Endangered Species of Wild Flora and Fauna (CITES) Appendix I, giving protection from international trade in most countries where the jaguar occurred, reduced the *reported* number of traded skins to very low levels by the mid-1970s, although some authorities feared that the *actual* number of traded skins was still high.

WHAT'S AHEAD FOR THE JAGUAR?

Although the legal trade in jaguar skins has declined dramatically, the skins are still illegally traded. The exact extent of this illegal trade (in a number of spotted cat species from Latin America, not just jaguar) is hard to ascertain for obvious reasons. But as long as strong financial incentives remain, so will this illegal commerce.

Additionally, jaguars are still taken in considerable numbers to protect domestic livestock. Rural people may take them for that reason, or opportunistically for sale at local levels for use in ceremonies, or just for bragging rights. Jaguars seem much more likely to prey on domestic livestock than do pumas and most of the other big cats. Adding to their woes is the fact that jaguars are also relatively easy to trap or poison.

Today, deforestation for timber, mineral, or agricultural purposes probably has the greatest impact on the jaguar. On the plus side, jaguar still inhabit huge tracts of remote rainforest in South America and certain small but rich core areas in Central America. However, these South American rainforest areas are being degraded at a rapid and increasing rate.

Thus it continues. Another big cat sorely beset as we roll it back fourteen hundred miles (2,240km) northward of its most southerly penetration in the recent past and one thousand miles (1,600km) south of his northern apogee. Furthermore, the jaguar's range is ever more discontinuous within these remaining limits, and its numbers are ever less dense within the remaining "inkblot" populations. The collision seems inevitable, the sad demise of wild, free-ranging populations foreordained. Can we set aside enough land from more intensive, "useful" usages and protect these areas from the ever-increasing human tribe over the long range so that *Panthera onca* can roam free? Time, priorities for the allocation of resources and shifting geopolitical realities will tell. Meanwhile, sturdy, stolid *onca* remains with us, wild and free for another brief moment. We are the better for his presence. ∎

Top: A three-toed sloth moves leisurely through the trees. A wonderful bon-bon for the jaguar when the cat (photo below) can spot the slow-moving, well-camouflaged sloth.

The jaguar has larger, heavier teeth and jaw muscles than its more northern neighbor the puma, and, where the two overlap, the jaguar uses these to good advantage to feed on a much higher percentage of turtles, tortoises, and spectacled caimans. In some areas, up to 30 percent of the jaguar's diet is comprised of these "hard-skinned" animals. A study by Louise Emmons, a research associate of the Smithsonian Institution Division of Mammals, found that in areas where all three cats overlap, the much smaller ocelot preyed mostly (92 percent) on animals weighing one kilogram (2.2lb.) or less, the jaguar targeted quarry that mostly (85 percent) weighed more than one kilogram (2.2lb.), and puma's prey analyzed in this study fell in the region where the jaguar and ocelot diet overlapped, one to ten kilograms (2.2–22lbs.). These prey patterns reflect not only the jaguar's larger size but also its more massive musculature.

Physical Characteristics
Size and Weight
The jaguar is the largest of the cats found in the Western Hemisphere and, along with the tiger, the lion, and the leopard, it is one of the four roaring or "great" cats.

On average, the jaguar is the third largest of the thirty-seven cats, exceeded in size by only the tiger and the lion, but as with its close relative the leopard, it shows enormous variation in size throughout its range. Maximum size is three hundred to 350 pounds (135–158kg), and minimum size is one hundred to 125 pounds (45–56kg), with females on average running 20 percent smaller. The jaguar's length is six to nine feet (1.8–2.7m), which includes a tail of twenty-seven inches (67.5cm). The tail is much shorter than the somewhat smaller but more agile puma of the Western Hemisphere. This is a compact, heavily muscled animal that exudes a solid power, unlike the more lithe, supple grace of most of the other big cats.

Pelage
The jaguar wears a beautiful spotted coat, which has worked to its severe detriment until recent years. Its basic color is yellow to tawny lightening to white on the belly and the insides of the legs. There is extensive variation in the coat patterns of both the leopard and the jaguar, and their pelts cannot always be distinguished. However, the leopard's rosettes are generally smaller and without dark markings in the center, while the jaguar has fewer, larger rosettes with additional black spots enclosed in most of the rosettes. The jaguar's skin is tighter than the puma's, and there is no slackness in the belly area as is common with the latter. The head is massive and rounded with small, rounded ears without terminal tufts.

All-black or melanistic jaguars occur in some areas, though

even on these black jaguars the spots can still be seen in the right light. Black leopards generally follow "Gloger's Rule," which states that dark color in mammals occurs more frequently in warm humid regions. J. J. Von Tschudi and Hans Krieg as well as many other researchers feel that this also applies to jaguar. However, author Richard Perry discounts this, saying that records indicate that black jaguars may outnumber the spotted variety in the drier areas of northeastern Brazil. Albinos or partial albinos are reputed to have occurred in Paraguay. ■

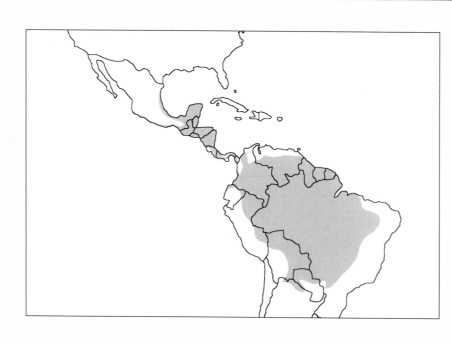

The Range of the Jaguar
(*Panthera onca*)

Facing page: *Although jaguar are thought of as forest animals, they have also survived and thrived in many harsh, subdesert areas. Bottom: Here, a jaguar is compared to its similar-looking but much smaller felid neighbor, the ocelot (top photo). Overleaf: Jaguars are the most water-loving big cat of all, and they thrive in extremely wet areas such as swamps.*

Evolution of the Jaguar

Jaguars evolved in Eurasia from a leopard ancestor and, about 1.6 million years ago, spread into North America via the Bering Land Bridge that once connected the present-day areas of Alaska and Siberia. These Pleistocene jaguars were much larger and longer-legged than modern jaguars. The largest and earliest fossils come from the northern United States (Nebraska, Oregon, and Washington), while the younger, smaller, and shorter-legged fossils of about 100,000 years ago are from more southern states, indicating a contraction of the jaguar's range over time. During the Pleistocene era, the reduction in jaguar's overall size and the shortening of the legs probably occurred as more open habitats were replaced by forest.

Paleontologists still disagree about these early jaguars. Some researchers have noted that the early jaguar is so similar to the modern jaguar, despite the size difference, that it is only a subspecies of the modern jaguar, and therefore named the early jaguar *Panthera onca augusta*. Others such as Theodore Galush have argued that *Panthera augusta* (as he has named the cat) remained a distinct species, temporarily overlapped by modern-day *Panthera onca* but eventually replaced by it. These big Pleistocene jaguars were never as large as the giant North American lion, *Panthera atrox*, of the same period, and generally occurred in different geographic regions. Few lions have been found in the Florida deposits where many specimens of *Panthera augusta* have been found, and researcher George Jefferson has only recently discovered a few bones of fossil jaguars in the Rancho LaBrea Tarpits of southern California, which preserved a large series of *Panthera atrox*. This suggests that they may have competed for the same prey, but each had an advantage over the other in different habitat.

It is not clear how late jaguars existed in the southeastern part of the United States. One of the more intriguing conjectures is based on some jaguar bones and footprints George G. Simpson found in a cave in Tennessee. After reviewing some legends of a great cat other than the puma in the Mississippi River valley, Simpson concludes that there is a faint chance that jaguars survived in the eastern part of the United States after the start of European settlement of the continent. ■

The jaguar can climb surprisingly well for such a heavy-weight.

116

Tigres that Recently Existed in Northwest Mexico and the Southwest United States

Researchers Stanley Young and Edward Goldman recognized sixteen subspecies of jaguar (*tigre* in Spanish), in a 1933 review; however, most authorities now support the eight subspecies recognized by E. R. Hall and K. R. Kelson in 1959. Two of these are of particular interest to U.S. observers.

A jaguar subspecies common in Texas until about 1870, when settlement and houndsmen who were employed by ranching interests sent the jaguar into a precipitous decline, was *Panthera onca veraecrucis*. This cat was found in the mid-1800s along watercourses in the region of San Antonio. General Sam Houston, president of the Republic of Texas when independence was declared from Mexico in 1836, reported it "abundant on the headwaters of the eastern tributaries of the Rio Grande, the Guadalupe, etc." By 1900, a writer by the name of Bailey reported the species as being scarce within the state. However, at that time the range of the species still had not declined much, as jaguars were reported around the turn of the century in such scattered locations as Jasper in eastern Texas, around Center City, and near the mouth of the Pecos River in southwestern Texas.

After the turn of the century, the jaguar all but disappeared from Texas, with only three records in recent years: one killed in 1946 in Cameron County, the southernmost county in Texas; one in Kleberg County in 1948; and an animal that is suspected of being a released captive killed near the town of Presidio in 1963. An occasional straggler may wander into Texas from Coahuila, Mexico, but the jaguar in Texas may now be assumed to be extirpated as a breeding population. According to Dennis Russell, who studied the status of these cats in Texas, it is unlikely that the jaguar could ever return to Texas because of the destruction of the subtropical brushlands near the border.

Panthera onca arizonenis ranged relatively recently throughout northwestern Mexico and into adjacent parts of the United States. Historic records indicate that most of this subspecies that lived in New Mexico were confined to the southwestern part of that state, and although occasional animals are reported there, there are no verified records for New Mexico since around the turn of the century. A tally of reports has shown that at least sixty-four jaguars have been killed in Arizona on other than guided hunts since 1900. The locations ranged from the southeastern border to as far north as the Grand Canyon. Because we know that the last indication of breeding populations of jaguars in the United States occurred in Arizona in the 1960s, it is assumed that the occasional jaguars killed in Arizona in 1971, 1980, and 1986 were strays from Mexico. The 1986 shooting occurred in the Dos Cabezas in the southeastern corner of Arizona, where the cat was hunted down by a rancher with dogs, killed, and taken to the nearby ranching community of Willcox; there it was seen by a dozen people and photographed.

Jaguars hung on longer in northern Mexico, but they are now largely gone from that area as well. They were still relatively common in the Mexican state of Sonora near the California-Arizona-Mexico border in the 1930s and the 1940s, when Dale and Clell Lee, professional cat hunters from Tucson, guided a number of paying hunters to them. Since Mexican authorities now report that the most northerly population of jaguars is eight hundred miles (1,280km) south of the U.S. border, where did that jaguar come from that was killed in Arizona in 1986? Did it wander nearly a thousand miles (1,600km) north, or was there a macro population of breeding jaguars in Sonora as recently as the late 1980s? ■

PUMA:
ATHLETE OF THE AMERICAS

THE SLEEK, SUPPLE MONTANA CAT LOWERED ITSELF SLIGHTLY, COCKED THE SHORT, ROUNDED EARS on its smallish, intelligent-looking face, and with a flowing ripple seemed to almost float up into the tree. Fifteen vertical feet up (4.5m) it landed with a fluid grace, completely belying the high-impact force of its 150 pounds (67.5kg), landing suddenly on the large tree limb. How easy it all looked. ■ The relatively long hind legs of the puma (*Felis concolor*) give it a tremendous leaping power. It can bound along at high speed and easily leap up into the crotch of a tree, usually about six feet (1.8m) off the ground, then climb up to sixty feet (18m) into the tree and make itself quite at home. Researcher C. T. Barnes wrote in 1960 that "... probably no other cat in the world can equal it in ease and resilience of spring. It can vault over the highest fences, bound safely down from incredibly high cliffs, and even plunge, as if it were some mammoth flying squirrel, into a labyrinth of tree tops; for, not being so heavy as either the African lion or the Indian tiger, nor so stocky as the leopard, it can excel them all in the grace and distance of its magnificent leaps... I have ... seen it jump from a branch to the earth 50 or 60 feet (15–18m) below and light on its feet apparently unhurt." ■ Over the years, big cat admirers have hoisted tribute after tribute to the puma's bounding ability for both horizontal and vertical leaps. In the 1880s, Clinton Hart Merriam, the U.S. Biological Survey scientist known for his "life zones" theory of plant communities, measured the distance of a puma's leap—sixty feet

*A puma (*Felis concolor*) pauses momentarily at a beaver pond where it has come to drink.*

Above: *The puma swims well, though unlike the jaguar, it generally shows an aversion to water, except in Florida where it will readily travel through shallow, flooded swamps.* Right: *The cougar's fluid grace is readily apparent here.*

(18m) to the ground from a ledge of rocks that was some twenty feet (6m) above the ground. One authority records thirty-nine feet (11.7m) as its longest known jump on the level; compare that to the world record for a man held by Carl Lewis—twenty-eight feet, ten and a quarter inches (8.65m). The researcher also wrote of an instance of a "measured leap over snow of nearly 40 feet [12m]." In 1920, a cat watcher by the name of Tinsley said that he once saw a puma bound into the fork of a tree twelve feet (3.6m) above the ground *with the carcass of a deer in its mouth*, and C. T. Barnes cited a height of eighteen feet (5.4m) for a puma's upward leap when the cat was not encumbered in any way. In another instance, a puma at rest on a slight downslope bolted thirteen feet (3.9m) from a standing start when it was startled.

Such is the supple strength of the puma, possibly the most agile athlete of all the big cats. The Montana athlete I witnessed on that late winter afternoon fluidly sprang into the tree, looked around, then bounded down off the other side as if, once he got there, he decided he didn't want to be there after all. Among the big cats only the snow leopard, which is built very similarly, rivals the puma for this kind of leaping and bounding athletic prowess.

THE RANGE OF THE PUMA

Pumas have the longest north-to-south distribution of any large mammal on earth, reaching over nine thousand miles (14,400km) from the southern tip of South America into isolated pockets of the southern Yukon and southeastern Alaska. What is more, although we know little about population size and status of the puma in Latin America, we do know that in North America pumas are increasing both their range and numbers.

The puma is, along with the typical leopard, among the most

adaptable of the big cats. Not only do pumas inhabit this huge swath of territory, but also they can live any place within this area where adequate cover exists for them to stalk game.

Contrary to popular myth, most of their kills are made by stalking, not ambush. They have lived and prospered in forests, swampy jungles, tropical forests, open grasslands, dry bush, semideserts, and alpine areas. They have been recorded from sea level to 14,800 feet (2,960m), thus practically matching the leopard in adaptability.

This species is unique among the big cats in that its future, at least in northern latitudes, is directly linked with the success of managing large and growing populations, rather than shrinking populations and ranges.

Human attitudes toward the puma have undergone a radical and remarkable transition in the last forty years, and this has greatly benefited the big cat. The challenge of the future will be to recognize that this is a highly efficient, dynamic, potentially dangerous predator, and then, taking that into account, to manage it for overall best effect for the species without allowing misplaced sentimentality for specific individual cats (and resultant attacks or negative incidents) to endanger the current public acceptance of the animal.

The puma, though not as spectacular as some of the other big cats, is an intelligent, highly adaptable predator that, along with the wolves and the bears, adds an excitement to the U.S. wildlands that simply would not be there in their absence. They are a remarkably athletic animal by any yardstick, and, as long as we treat them with the respect that they deserve, the outlook for this big cat is uniquely positive. ∎

What is a Puma?

Authorities are divided over the taxonomic identity of the puma. The first scientific recognition of the puma occurred in 1771, when Swedish botanist and creator of our scientific naming system Carolus Linnaeus described a new species, *Felis concolor* (cat of one color), based on a skin brought back from French Guiana. At that time and according to his usage, the genus name *Felis* covered all cats.

In 1834 Sir William Jardine proposed a separate genus, *Puma*, for the puma and several smaller cats. Subsequent authorities, upon further investigation of the smaller cats such as the jaguarundi (*Felis yagouaroundi*) and ocelot (*Felis pardalis*), have disagreed with Jardine's grouping, and adhere to Linneaus's original classification. Some biologists consider the puma to be different enough from the smaller cats to warrant its own separate genus, but that change has not been made. There is no doubt that the puma resembles many of the smaller cats in several respects, and differs from many of the big cats. Due to a different anatomy in the throat, it cannot roar, as can four of the five pantherine cats (lion, tiger, leopard, and jaguar—the snow leopard cannot). Furthermore, the general shape of *Felis concolor*'s skull is somewhat different from that of the other big cats. Pumas resemble the smaller cats and other cats in the genus *Felis* in having a shorter, wider skull with a relatively expanded braincase and a shorter "face" or snout—the distance from the eye sockets to the end of the muzzle. Furthermore, the puma's head is small in relation to its body size when compared with that of the other big cats.

Daniel B. Adams has recently suggested that the puma's closest relative among the living cats may be the cheetah. Indeed, the puma resembles the cheetah in its relatively small head and moderately long limbs. And Adams's suggestion is somewhat supported by the characteristics of a large ancestral puma, *Felis inexpectata,* which lived in North America from one to three million years ago. As with most cats and other mammals of that era, these ancestral puma were ten to 30 percent larger than the modern puma. (The oldest fossils assigned to the modern puma date back as far as three hundred thousand years in North America and are the same size as today's puma.) Also, they were longer-legged and more cursorial, thus more similar to the modern cheetah, than to the current, modern puma.

However, most authorities insist that it is unclear which of the other cats the puma is most closely related to. The overall evidence suggests that the puma has evolved from a separate lineage that diverged before the diversification of most of the other modern cats.■

The Range of the Puma (*Felis concolor*)

Above: *A puma that definitely means business. Note the whiskers extended forward and the laid-back ears.* Far right: *A puma mom carries her kitten to a safer location.* Right: *The puma can breed at any time during the year, thus these cubs in winter snow. This is highly unusual among large mammals.*

Pumas versus Humans: A Changing Trend

Within the city of Boulder, Colorado, just twenty miles (32km) north of Denver with a population of about eighty thousand, wild pumas have given birth to kittens beneath the porches of private homes. In Loveland, Colorado, a community of about thirty-seven thousand located thirty miles (48km) northeast of Boulder, alarmed parents fenced an elementary school playground when a puma was sighted sitting near the schoolyard in broad daylight, intently studying the children at play. In 1991 in Idaho Springs, Colorado, fifty miles (80km) southwest of Boulder, a high school senior, Scott Lancaster, jogged home, following a trail often used for that purpose. Hours later, searchers found a puma crouched over his partially consumed body. Elsewhere are other "hot spots" of puma-human encounters, such as Big Bend National Park in Texas, and Orange County, California, where multiple attacks have occurred. What is happening?

Puma-human encounters are not recent phenomena: In 1986 Lee Fitzhugh and partners presented a summary of sixty-six recorded attacks by pumas against people throughout the puma's range dating from 1750, and undoubtedly not all incidents were recorded. Fewer than half the attacks were fatal, but the injuries were often serious. Since 1986, additional attacks have occurred. In a five-month period of 1990, there were twenty puma-human encounters (not attacks, per se) in the Flathead Valley of Montana. In 1990, there were seventy-nine potentially serious puma-human incidents in Boulder County, Colorado, in which researchers believed humans were—or could have been—attacked or injured. Twenty-three of these incidents occurred on the porches of suburban homes and eight happened in driveways; in one case, a playful cat was found on the roof toying with a weather vane.

Although these figures have to be put into context, it's worth asking, What can explain the apparently accelerating rate of puma-human incidents? It should be emphasized that pumas do not begin to approach such other big cats as tigers, leopards, or jaguars in frequency of attacks on humans. For instance, in a single year in the mid-1980s tigers are known to have killed more than 150 people in India. When you allow for additional unreported tiger kills, plus many additional tiger attacks not resulting in human fatalities, the total number of attacks is "impressive" indeed. That number of attacks on humans occurred even though there are only about as many tigers in India as there are pumas in California. Nor, taking numbers and behavior into account, can pumas be seen to be anywhere near as dangerous as the far smaller populations of grizzly bears located in the lower forty-eight United States. Yet the worrisome thing is that there is no denying that the number of puma attacks on humans in the U.S. is increasing. The reasons become readily evident upon closer consideration.

The core of this situation is based on the decisions of many communities regarding land use. People have chosen to live in areas of abundant wildlife, and have taken steps such as maintaining low-density housing, abundant open space, and restraints on hunting to ensure that animals flourish. With increased numbers of both pumas and people around, the chances of pumas encountering people have dramatically increased. With each encounter that ends in no harm to the puma, that puma loses much of its fear of people, and possibly even begins to associate people with food.

In addition to human encroachment into prime puma habitat, overall puma numbers may be an all-time high (although some professionals disagree). A large part of this is because primary puma prey, such as mule deer, whitetailed deer, and elk are also at high numbers. Also, pumas have been receiving much stronger legal protection by the removal of bounty programs and the restriction of legal killing during the past twenty years or so.

There is no consensus as to why certain "hot spot" areas such as Boulder County, some areas in Montana (mainly in the Flathead Valley), and southern California have

124

emerged. It may be that there is an overpopulation of pumas in these areas, and natural selection is favoring the more aggressive cats. It may also be that some cats might be altering their habit of following deer to the high mountain summer ranges in order to remain near valley communities and prey on suburban dogs, domestic cats, and other domestic stock. It is logical that if pumas become hungry, they will eat a greater variety of prey.

People are usually not prey for pumas, and attacks on people have been rare when compared with the opportunities. Prey recognition is a learned behavior in cats, and knowledge of what constitutes prey can be gained in a number of ways. Predators do not consider every animal they come across as prey; however, several encounters with a strange species may lead the cat to identify that species as prey. Alternatively, one puma can learn from another that a strange animal is prey, if the two are together at the time of an attack. Typical innate feline behavior is

to attack anything that moves rapidly, especially away or at right angles. This is especially true during breeding cycles when hormonal levels are high.

Another prey-identification method, according to a somewhat controversial theory, is that if the drive for prey-catching is interrupted or unsuccessful, the cat must "vent" its drive. Thus, if a puma encounters a human just after an unsuccessful attempt to catch prey, the behavior may be transferred to the human. Normally pumas are stimulated to attack by any animal (including humans) of normal prey size that exhibits prey behavior such as flight, quick movements, and, probably for children in small groups, excited conversation. Before pumas apply this behavior to people, several encounters may be required for the individual puma to classify humans as prey. Captive pumas have frequently shown heightened interest, and in some cases, exhibited attack behavior, toward human children while ignoring nearby human adults, perhaps because the children are closer in size to recognized prey species.

Just as attitudes and programs were altered when puma numbers fell to historic lows, such changes may again be necessary as they climb to all-time highs. The first step is to identify higher hazard areas. One indicator of higher risk situations is heavy individual human use of areas where pumas are resident in large numbers. High puma populations near urban areas should be a cause for increased alertness. In these "hot spot" areas, it is necessary to admit that there is a problem and that it is one that will probably increase in severity unless appropriate measures are taken, regardless of the emotional issues involved.

Management options to prevent attacks include warnings, limiting human use, removing pumas, and modifying habitat. Warnings should be direct and severe. Pumas are not animals to be taken lightly, and people should be told forcefully that they can be dangerous. Limitations on human use of "hot spots" can be partial, complete, or time-specific. One successful limitation applied in Orange County, California, restricted use of trails in the Ronald W. Caspers Wilderness Park to

groups of people eighteen years old and older. No attacks have occurred since this restriction. Hunting is not the only way of removing pumas, but it is the most cost-effective. In some areas and situations, well-managed and tightly monitored hunting may be advisable. Hunting does not seem appropriate in suburban areas where children, in particular, may be at risk. Practical habitat modifications usually involve extensive removal of cover around trails or high-risk areas (such as campgrounds).

Once a puma attack has occurred, all possible resources should be applied to locating and removing that specific cat, in one fashion or another, since another attack is almost sure to occur. Predictably, there is often a strong emotional response against any sort of hunting or removal of puma. Not all environmentalists are against it, though. Hank Fischer, Northern Rockies representative for Defenders of Wildlife, said his organization has taken no position on Montana pumas, and he anticipates none. In fact, Fischer has said he is personally confused about the animal. "I'm an adult making adult choices, going into grizzly habitat, knowing an encounter could happen and willing to accept the results. Mountain lions are something else. If they're coming into residential areas, stalking or preying on children, there just seems to be something more sinister about that."

Living with and continuing to maintain high populations of pumas will require changing approaches and attitudes, just as changes were required in human attitudes when puma populations were at an all-time low. Maurice Hornocker, dean of puma experts, has said: "We're dealing with a great carnivore success story. Perhaps the only one!" The puma is a highly adaptable, successful, lethal predator. The vast majority of people want this animal to prosper and maintain populations within the limits of available habitat and prey-availability. To do this will call for increasingly sophisticated research and public reaction in order to avoid future negative overreaction if puma-human incidents and attacks are allowed to continually increase due to well-intentioned, but unsound, attitudes. ■

Left: A puma alert in heavy cover. Overleaf: This coyote continually worried a puma with its fresh deer kill until the fretful cat had been teased into chasing it away. The puma will not be able to catch the smaller, more nimble coyote if the latter stays alert.

Physical Characteristics
Size and Weight

Pumas can be distinguished from other cats by the combination of large size, slender form, long cylindrical tail, short ears, and plain color of adults. Pumas are distinctly different from lions—the other single-color big cat—in skull size, relative proportions of limbs, ability to roar (the puma cannot), method of feeding, and in a number of other fundamental ways.

Pumas range in length from about five and one-half feet to eight and one-half feet (1.7–2.6m), of which up to twenty-eight inches (70cm) is tail length. Shoulder height averages twenty-seven inches (67.5cm), and adult males are about 40 percent larger than adult females.

While average adult weights range from sixty pounds to 225 pounds (27–101kg), depending upon the location and sex of the cat, and season of the year, much larger pumas have been recorded, such as the very heavy 265-pound (119-kg) male puma that was killed in Utah. The heaviest puma yet recorded was killed in Arizona and weighed 275.4 pounds (124kg) with the intestines removed. That cat had to weigh over three hundred pounds (135kg) intact, perhaps considerably more.

As with most other large mammals, the average size of individuals generally increases as they move further from the equator. A detailed study by B. Kurten in 1973 demonstrated the interesting fact that while size increases evenly with latitude as puma move both north and south away from the equator, the teeth increase in size more toward the south, especially in males, so that individuals from southern Argentina have distinctly larger teeth than similarly sized northern pumas located about the same distance away from the equator.

Pelage

The adult puma's coat ranges from a plain gray-brown or reddish to almost black. Reddish cats are more prevalent in tropical regions, and black has been noted once in southern South America.

Felis concolor's coat is short and bristly in tropical regions and longer and softer in the north. The sides of its muzzle are black; the undersides, chin, and throat are almost pure white. Puma kittens are distinctly spotted but lose those markings as they mature. (Because pumas are not considered to be one of the "great" cats, their young are called kittens, not cubs.) ∎

Above: Winter is the time of hardship for all animals. Here a hungry puma has surprised a young beaver and overcome its own aversion to water as it attacks the beaver in its frigid pond. Left: A mated pair of pumas. Note the much larger size of the male.

The Names of the Puma

The puma carries probably more common names than any other cat: cougar, puma, mountain lion, catamount (from "cat-o'-mountain"), deer tiger, painter, panther, American lion, Mexican lion, red jaguar, silver lion, mountain screamer, and king cat are but a few of them. Central and South Americans use *chimblea, miztil, pagi, leon,* and *leopardo*. One of the more fascinating historical names for the puma comes from Argentina and translates to "friend of man." Most scientific literature uses the common name "puma" to refer to this cat. ■

How the Puma Hunts

The colloquial name "deer tiger" is a good one for the puma since, throughout its range, deer make up such a major portion of its diet. In the northern latitudes, this means mule deer, whitetailed deer, blacktailed deer, and elk. In South America, pumas prey heavily on small Brocket deer.

A chief limitation on the puma's range is lack of cover, which they need to stalk prey. Cat researchers such as Stanley Young and Edward Goldman have watched the puma's deadly style. Rather than lying in wait, the puma actively stalks its prey, cautiously remaining under cover and undetected until within striking distance. The puma uses its tremendous bounding capabilities when it is close enough, leaping on its target and knocking it to the ground by the force of its attack. Death is caused by a swift, killing bite.

According to several eyewitness accounts, the cat generally leaps onto the back of the victim and fixes its claws into the prey's neck or shoulders. Maurice G. Hornocker of the University of Idaho, who surveyed tracks made in snow during attempted attacks, reports about 80 percent of the attacks to be successful. However, the degree of success in the preliminary phases—locating and stalking quarry—has been impossible to quantify but must be considerably less.

As with most cats, pumas are very opportunistic and will take smaller prey when they can. Also, young pumas are often too unskilled or not large enough to successfully hunt adult deer, while old adult pumas with worn canines, arthritis, or injuries may become physically incapable of bringing down such large prey. Smaller prey can include ground squirrels, beavers, skunks, rabbits, armadillos, peccaries, rodents such as pacas and agoutis, turkeys, alligators, and even carrion. One puma was observed making a meal on grasshoppers.

Porcupines can be a significant prey for some pumas, who learn to avoid the formidable array of quills by flipping the animal over onto its back and then ripping into the unprotected abdomen. Pumas do have to be careful, though: Quills do cause serious injury if they become embedded in the cat's lips, tongue, palate, or facial muscles.

Puma take livestock when natural prey is scarce or absent. Livestock killing is one of the principal causes of human aggression against pumas. Pumas may take not only calves, pigs, sheep, goats, and even full-grown cattle, but are especially fond of horses and burros. Because pumas do attack large prey violently, they are themselves occasionally killed during these encounters, and researchers have reported that pumas have been killed by burros, bull and cow elk, and buck deer. They also suffer accidental deaths, primarily by being struck by cars. Pumas also kill bobcats, more for spite than for food. In South America they tend to avoid lowland or water areas when jaguar are present. ∎

Above: A puma confronts a plucky badger. This stout weasel stood his ground successfully. Bottom left: A coyote warily circles a cougar with a deer kill. Although the coyote cannot take the kill away from the cat, he is too quick to be caught by the larger competitor. Bottom right: Some pumas learn to safely kill porcupines. However, to do it incorrectly could be very painful—even fatal—for the cat.

Left: *A rare Florida panther, also called an eastern puma (Felis concolor coryi). Right: This eight-week-old cougar, sprawling awkwardly on a dead branch, hardly hints at the athletic grace to come.*

Subspecies of Puma

Pumas demonstrate considerable variation in size and color, partially due to their very wide distribution both geographically and by type of habitat. This has led to the assignment of as many as twenty-four to thirty subspecies by different authorities. As with most other cats, some subspecies were based on very few specimens and would be difficult to justify.

The Florida Panther

There is much current interest in the United States regarding *Felis concolor coryi*, the puma of the southeast, the so-called "Florida panther." Long limbs, small feet, and rich reddish (rather than gray) color distinguish this subspecies. In common with most cat species, this race of puma, because it lives in subtropical regions, is generally darker in color than its subdesert, dry-country counterparts. Although about five hundred wild pumas still existed in Florida at the beginning of this century, they have steadily declined in the face of expanding human populations and activities. In 1991, biological administrator David S. Maehr of the Florida Game and Fresh Water Fish Commission estimated at least seventy-five wild Florida panthers remained in southern Florida.

A Species Survival Plan (SSP) for the Florida panther was developed in 1989 at meetings of specialists and under the auspices of the International Union for the Conservation of Nature (IUCN). This plan envisages the establishment of a breeding population—a combination of 130 wild and captive pumas—by the year 2000, increasing to five hundred breeding-age panthers by the year 2010. Currently, twenty-four wild *coryi* are monitored with radio collars as part of the intensive research program underway on this highly en-

dangered subspecies.

Some Florida panthers face several other threats in addition to the lack of genetic diversity inherent in such a small population. Extremely high levels of mercury were found in the liver of a panther that died in southern Florida's Everglades in the summer of 1989. Over one hundred parts per million were found, whereas the level at which the U.S. Food and Drug Administration can initiate legislation or restrictions is only one part per million.

Although warnings about mercury levels in fish have already been issued in some parts of Florida, Dennis Jordan, the Florida panther coordinator of the Florida Cooperative Fish and Wildlife Research Unit, said that none of the usual sources of mercury contamination were found in the state, and one hypothesis suggested (although no one really knows) that the mercury could be coming from a natural source—the peat and muck soils that are common throughout Florida. These are often flooded and provide a suitable environment for production of methylmercury, the biologically active and toxic form of mercury, from inorganic mercury, which is considered biologically innocuous. Fortunately mercury is not a problem for most panthers since the core population is in southwest Florida.

On the plus side, *Felis concolor coryi* is receiving strong support of various types. From 1983 to 1984, four panthers were killed by cars on Alligator Alley, which cuts through the Everglades in the heart of the Florida panther's habitat. The federal government agreed in 1986 to construct thirty-six underpasses beneath Interstate 75 (which replaced Alligator Alley as the main east–west road across southern Forida). Furthermore, fences were built to keep them from wandering onto the road. Maehr commented that recent studies

show panthers readily use these underpasses.

In January 1990 John F. Eisenberg of the University of Florida stated that "I am happy to report that there are more Florida panthers than previously estimated. . . ." In an attempt to test reintroduction possibilities, seven pumas brought in from Texas (not of the *Felis concolor coryi* subspecies) were radio-collared and released into Osceola National Forest in northern Florida. At the conclusion of the twelve-month study, four of these panthers were recaptured; two had been shot. The seventh was unaccounted for and presumed dead. The results indicated that all four did quite well, with two of them actually gaining weight.

Although a number of sightings have been reported, there is no strong evidence to support the existence of *coryi* in portions of northeastern Alabama, possibly portions of western Louisiana, and northern Georgia, although pumas did once live in these places. A three-year study funded by the U.S. Fish and Wildlife Service also found no sign of puma in Arkansas. All previous "evidence" was found to be second- and third-hand reports of sightings.

Other Puma Subspecies

Puma authority Ronald Hall has recognized fifteen subspecies of puma north of South America; of these, ten have some or all of their range in the United States west of the Mississippi River and in the westernmost Canadian provinces. Obviously, their ranges do not coincide with political lines, but following are the latest estimates by political units:

Alberta—no estimate
Arizona—2,000

British Columbia—2,280 to 3,800
California—5,100
Colorado—3,000 and increasing
Idaho—1,800
Montana—no population figures available, but the population is undoubtedly increasing
Nevada—800, and currently at or near an all-time high
New Mexico—2,000
Oregon—no estimate
Texas—65 to 125, with 30 in Big Bend National Park
Utah—1,500
Washington—1,500
Wyoming—1,000

As with estimates for populations of all big cats, it should be emphasized that these free-ranging, furtive animals are among the most difficult of all to estimate, and all figures are, at best, educated guesses. Pumas are known to be expanding their range northward and eastward, especially into the southern third of the Yukon; a portion of northern Saskatchewan; north, south, and west of Lake Winnipeg, Manitoba; extreme southwest Ontario; and northern Minnesota.

Taken in the context of the preceding editorial caveat about such estimates, it is interesting to note that these figures total over twenty thousand—perhaps the actual number is well over that mark. That total does not include estimates for a number of areas such as Montana, Oregon, Alberta, and other possible pockets of puma territory. It is possible there are more than thirty thousand wild pumas alive today north of the Mexican border. ∎

CLOUDED LEOPARD: SPLENDOR IN THE TREES

THE CLOUDED LEOPARD (*NEOFELIS NEBULOSA*) IS A CAT OF EXTREMES AND SUPERLATIVES. THE FIRST time I saw one, I could scarcely believe my eyes. Its coat was so lustrous and magnificently marked, its long body was set up on such short, stubby legs, and punctuated by the longest canine teeth (relative to body size) up front and the longest tail (relative to body size) at the back. This was a captive cat; since few, if any, Westerners have ever seen this animal in the wild. In fact, I cannot find any reference of anyone, other than perhaps a few villagers who also live in the cat's Southeast Asian range, who has seen one of these most secretive, heavy-cover animals in the wild. Very little is known about this arboreal cat in the wild, and what little we have discovered has mostly been found in the last five years. One thing we do know: The clouded leopard is, arguably, the most beautiful of all the world's thirty-seven felids. *Arguably* is the key word here—since there is probably more spirited debate regarding this animal's beauty versus that of other cats than any mentioned in this book. Unfortunately, we probably know less about this cat than any of the others featured in this book. ■ John Lewis, director of the John Ball Zoological Gardens and International Studbook Keeper for the clouded leopard, commented about our unfamiliarity with this magnificent cat: "Our lack of knowledge about the clouded leopard's natural history and/or ecology is a threat since we cannot establish an effective protection policy without it. The species has never been considered plentiful, even in historical literature. Is that

The clouded leopard (Neofelis nebulosa) has unusually short legs which are part of its adaptation for life in the trees.

because they have very low population densities or because man has not discovered their true niche? I don't know."

There are no population estimates in the literature for any of the four originally recognized subspecies: *Neofelis nebulosa brachyurus* (the Taiwan clouded leopard), *Neofelis nebulosa nebulosa*, *Neofelis nebulosa macsceloides*, and *Neofelis nebulosa diardi*. Although Alan Rabinowitz has been conducting an extended study of the clouded leopard in Thailand from a field station based in the Huay Kha Wildlife Sanctuary (adjoining the Burmese border), we are still far from knowing its ecological and behavioral characteristics well enough to suggest specific measures for its conservation, except to emphasize the overriding need for forest protection.

This most beautiful of animals creates daunting conservation problems for a number of reasons: its preference for high forest as habitat; its large body size and consequent need for a relatively large home range; the high commercial value of its pelt, making commercial poaching very profitable and difficult to control; ready availability of poisons, particularly DDT, used in agricultural settlements surrounding game reserves to kill predators that might attack cattle and poultry; and demand for clouded leopard as a delicacy in some restaurants, particularly in China.

THE THREATENED CLOUDED LEOPARD

The clouded leopard's high forest habitat is under siege and shrinking at an astonishing rate. Most media attention is focused on tropical rainforests in Amazonia, when actually there are a number of areas throughout the world that are at risk, and the tropical forest areas of Southeast Asia are being cleared and decimated as fast as any on earth. Part of the jaguar's range in South America includes open plains and other less forested areas, so its overall survival is not quite so heavily locked into the core forest area. Such is not true of the tree-dwelling clouded leopard.

If conservation of this beautiful cat is to be truly effective, significant compromises relating to timber usage and consumption must be made by all of us. It has been found that logging per

se need not conflict with conservation of the clouded leopard, provided that it is strictly controlled and is limited to felling trees above fifty centimeters (20in.) in diameter at chest height. This sort of selective cutting is far more expensive than clear cutting. However, clear cutting, either for timber or to clear land for agricultural settlements, is disastrous to this animal.

Additional knowledge about methods to conserve the clouded leopard is urgently needed. Complicating efforts is the fact that this animal is extremely hard to study, due to its largely nocturnal and arboreal habits. In areas close to human settlement it becomes extremely cautious and exclusively nocturnal. Charles Santiapillai, an authority on the clouded leopard, also emphasizes the need for strict control of the use of poisons, together with conservation education at the grassroots level—so that adjacent peoples shed their traditional antipathy to predators and learn to regard them as important components of the ecosystem.

This magnificent little beast, smallest of the "large" cats, is a part of our world environmental heritage. It is no longer enough for us to say that *they*—the poorer, less-developed nations actually blessed with these cats—should conserve them. Such conservation inevitably involves costs—generally significant ones. Some are known, out-of-pocket costs to respective governments for protection patrols, education, and maintenance of sanctuary areas that cannot then be used more intensively for human purposes. Other costs are more indirect and are usually "paid" by the indigenous peoples living immediately adjacent to these cats—loss of wood for building and burning, loss of rights to hunt prey used by both the cats and by humans, and occasional losses of livestock to marauding cats.

Is it fair or even rational that these often poorer peoples should bear all or most of the costs? Especially when the trade-off for significant income from game viewing is not a possibility, as it is with the terrestrial cats of more open country, such as the cheetah and the lion, the leopard in many African locales, and the tiger in some of its Asian locales. We all want this cat. The question is, How much? ∎

Facing page: *A clouded leopard slakes its thirst on a hot day in the forest.* Above: *Today's growing demand for forest products at the lowest possible cost is putting the clouded leopard at risk. The cat's very arboreal nature and its need for high forest habitat puts it in direct competition with humans who are stripping the forests. Additionally, the clouded leopard's relatively large body size means that this animal needs a larger prey base and thus more area to sustain it. Overleaf: Two small kittens try out their "sea legs" up in the canopy where they will eventually learn to be supreme aerialists. Note the splendidly marked fur, even on these youngsters.*

There are approximately 273 clouded leopards alive today in the world's zoos, with possibly a similar number held in the private sector, and an unknown but small and declining number of them left in their wild range from southeastern Asia to southern China over into fringes of Nepal and India. Right: Again, note this cat's extremely short legs and the full-sized lower canines it has along with the large upper canines.

Physical Characteristics
Size and Weight
Clouded leopards form a bridge between the small cats and the other large cats. This is the smallest of the cats covered in this book, but even discussions about the clouded leopard's size cause disagreement. Some authorities indicate a maximum weight in the wild of forty to forty-five pounds (18–20kg) for males, while others add as much as 20 percent to that. Shoulder height is about twenty-one inches (52.5cm), just about half that of a good-sized tiger, and total length can range up to six and one-half feet (1.95m). The tail is well-furred and relatively heavy throughout its entire length, as well as comprising 45–50 percent of the total length of the cat. It functions as a balancing mechanism necessary for the cat's aerial acrobatics high up in the trees.

Pelage
The clouded leopard's coat, for which it is named, varies from brown to pale or rich yellowish-brown to white or pale tawny underneath. Its flanks are marked with large, irregularly disposed cloudy blotches darker in color than the background and partially edged in black. The glory and destruction of the clouded leopard is its fur, which sometimes brings more than $2,000 U.S. for a single skin on the black market in such places as Singapore. This is one of several severe difficulties faced by this animal in its fight for survival.

The Clouded Leopard's Teeth
This "cat of the trees" has some of the longest canine teeth, relative to its body size, of any felid—up to two inches (5cm). The clouded leopard has a remarkably long skull for a cat, with well-developed crests for the attachment of jaw muscles, undoubtedly related to its most striking characteristic. These teeth are such that at times the clouded leopard is compared to the long-extinct sabertoothed cats. However, these long canines differ considerably from those of the sabertoothed cats. The clouded leopard's canines are not bladelike, as was the case with the sabertooth's. Also, unlike the sabertooth's, the clouded leopard's lower canines are not reduced in size but, instead, are quite large. These big canines appear to be used for holding and killing large prey such as deer, wild pigs, and very large monkeys. The clouded leopard does sometimes take birds, but not as often as was thought when it was regarded as exclusively arboreal. In heavy forests, its principal prey is likely to be monkeys, and it is also known (in Borneo) to feed on orangutans. It is an opportunistic feeder, like all cats, and has occasionally been observed trying to catch fish in swamps. ∎

The Arboreal Clouded Leopard

Although somewhat awkward on the ground due to its short legs, the clouded leopard is graceful and supremely agile aloft. This is one of the most arboreal of all the cats, including even that sensational Western Hemisphere acrobat of the trees, the margay. However, current supposition is that the cat is somewhat more terrestrial than was originally thought.

Researcher Alan Rabinowitz suggested in preliminary surveys of the clouded leopard in Sabah and Sarawak in northern Borneo that, at least in these locations, the cat is not truly arboreal, and most likely uses trees primarily as resting sites. Other authorities strongly dispute this conclusion. In any event, there is no doubt that this cat is a supreme aerialist, being able to leap fifteen feet (4.5m) and more from one branch to

another with apparent ease. The clouded leopard can climb slowly down a vertical tree trunk head first, rather than descending like a domestic cat—hindquarters first and then turning to jump to the ground in the last meter. In addition to walking gracefully along the tops of branches, using that long, keel-like tail for balance, the clouded leopard can also traverse horizontal branches while hang-

ing *beneath* them like a sloth. It is even able to hang from a branch by its hind feet alone, letting its forequarters hang free. It is speculated that this is useful when it wants to drop straight down onto a deer or wild pig, thus ambushing such relatively large prey from above. ■

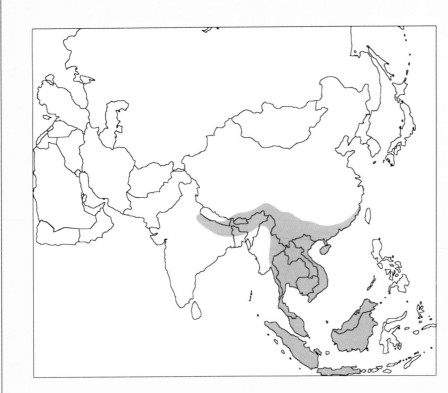

The Range of the Clouded Leopard (*Neofelis nebulosa*)

The Subspecies of Clouded Leopards

The clouded leopard is generally placed in its own separate, one-animal genus, *Neofelis*; similarly, the cheetah occupies its own genus, *Acinonyx*. This is because both of these animals are so specialized.

The clouded leopard (*Neofelis nebulosa*) was accorded four subspecies, but the Taiwan clouded leopard (*Neofelis nebulosa brachyurus*) is generally regarded as extinct. All the clouded leopard skins from Taiwan found in a recent survey were sixty years old and older. The newer skins were all smuggled in from mainland China. Though there are rumored sightings as recently as the 1960s, most authorities feel that the subspecies is now extinct on Taiwan.

Neofelis nebulosa nebulosa, the nominate subspecies, is found in southern China and throughout Indochina to eastern Myanmar (formerly Burma). It is characterized by a particularly rich coloration, and its coat is lighter, brighter, and more yellow than the other two living races, with more transversely elongated blotches.

Neofelis nebulosa macrosceloides is found from Nepal and its neighbor to the east, Sikkim, through portions of eastern India and Bangladesh to Myanmar. It can be distinguished from the other two varieties by its darker, grayer hue and larger blotches.

Neofelis nebulosa diardi is found on the Malay Peninsula and the Indonesian islands of Sumatra and Borneo. Its coloration is also darker and less yellow, but it is marked by smaller blotches, which are sometimes almost round or rosettelike. Before the turn of this century, when much of Sumatra was still covered with primary rainforest, the clouded leopard maintained substantial and continuous populations throughout this large island. Today, because of severe loss of habitat, the clouded leopard is found only in a few discontinuous areas. ■

Facing page: Looking at this clouded leopard kitten of about six weeks, it is difficult to say they should be denied a place to live in their high, wild tropical forests. Above: This clouded leopard's agile descent (more difficult than ascending) is accomplished with greater ease than many cats can climb the same branch. So little is known about the clouded leopard that about the only thing we know about its breeding is that females in the wild have been known to use standing trees with cavities as dens. The litter of two to five kittens is produced after a ninety-day gestation period.

One subspecies of clouded leopard, Neofelis nebulosa brachyurus, has been given a common name, Taiwan clouded leopard—although it is extinct. But, also perhaps because so little is known about the species in general, including exactly where it lives, zoologists have not given the other three subspecies common names.

SNOW LEOPARD: GHOST OF THE HEIGHTS

Snow leopard. The very name conjures up spectacle and drama. There's an apparent contradiction at work here: *Leopard* is a word we associate with the tropics, so that *snow* is, in a sense, its antithesis. ■ The first time I saw a snow leopard, my reaction was the same as most people's. I was astonished at the animal's beauty and marveled at its elegance of carriage as it padded around its zoo enclosure. "What is *that?*" I wanted to know as I tugged at my dad's hand. It was a striking impression from which I have never recovered—nor does most anyone else who sees this beast "up close and personal." This is not an animal about which one ever becomes blasé. Its appearance, athletic ability, spectacular home environment, and difficulty of making a living all conspire to put it near the top of anyone's "A" list of worldwide animals. ■ The snow leopard (*Panthera uncia*) is an almost mythical beast. Fabulously beautiful, it stands out even in this family of spectacularly attractive animals and is felt by many to be the most beautiful of the cats. It lives a solitary existence at altitudes mostly exceeding ten thousand feet (3,000m) and has been recorded as high as twenty thousand feet (6,000m). It can live, and hunt, as high as any prey species can exist. ■ Adding to the snow leopard's enigmatic quality is its ability to thrive in the most dramatically beautiful country on earth, making its living by hunting prey fully its equal in exotic beauty and rarity. It stalks the legendary Marco Polo sheep (one of the two longest-horned animals in the world) along with other huge argali sheep; it also hunts the

The enigmatic face of the snow leopard (Panthera uncia). If there ever was a "beautiful blond" among the big cats, this is the one!

grandest of the wild goats, the markhor and the ibex, and those curious originals, the Himalayan tahr and the bharal or blue sheep. Like all cats, it is opportunistic and will also take such "mundane" prey as marmots and pikas.

The country it lives in and prefers is certainly an appropriate backdrop for such a kingly beast. The snow leopard thrives in the highest, most remote mountains on earth outside of Antarctica. Its range stretches in an enormous arc that starts at the top in Mongolia and Russia and curves down through portions of Afghanistan, Pakistan, India, Nepal, and Bhutan, finally sweeping to the east throughout a giant swath of China, the extent of which has not been fully determined. Unfortunately, the central spine of this range exactly follows politically troubled border areas between several countries, complicating conservation and study efforts.

Although the snow leopard inhabits a vast range, populations are discontinuous and of thin density, due to the harshness of the habitat. Since this is some of the most difficult country on earth to travel in, censusing and detailed study is very difficult, although some promising studies are underway.

One such study is being conducted by Rodney Jackson of the California Institute of Environmental Studies, who has stated that he doubts that *Panthera uncia* is endangered throughout its range, although "the situation is very grave in Pakistan, Afghanistan, and Jammu and Kashmir, where endangered status is warranted." He further indicated that a range-wide assessment is urgently needed, and that he was developing a model for a "habitat suitability index" for the snow leopard, through which it "may be possible to make a range-wide estimate by extrapolation."

THE THREAT OF POACHING

The snow leopard is poached in some areas for the fur trade. Also, since much of its range lies in politically unstable areas with large military detachments of bored young men in uniform who possess automatic weapons and, it seems, a driving urge to use them on any wildlife they encounter, a further complication is added.

Another deep and abiding difficulty is cultural. As Eugene Koshkarev, a Russian academician, put it in a 1985 letter to the International Snow Leopard Trust: "Substantial obstacles in the path . . . are overcoming the carrier of tradition and habit existing in indigenous peoples in connection with hunting snow leopards. The issue is difficult to resolve for the reason that hunting snow leopards is often an integral part of the culture and life of the peoples themselves. Hunting traditions in various countries have established firm roots after many centuries of history. It is not accidental that . . . poaching in the present day remains critical."

The snow leopard is not alone in falling victim to its own charisma. India has, on balance, done a fine job of tiger conservation with generally meager resources and strong political difficulties in some areas. Yet when I was there in 1986, I found that even some high-ranking officers in the forestry department (which had jurisdiction over the national parks and Project Tiger reserves) were prone to try to poach a tiger, as has been the case with a limited number of other high political figures in India and extraordinarily wealthy royal visitors from abroad. The call of the past and a man's status as a true "man of the forest" was forever established by the killing of a tiger. In some quarters, high acclaim and social approbation still accompany tiger killing, even among generally "sophisticated" people. The situation does not approach wholesale proportions, but has occurred enough over recent years to be troubling.

Koshkarev's letter goes on to say, in regard to the snow leopard: "I would like to believe sincerely that mankind will not allow itself to deprive this beautiful, high-mountain cat of the right to live, and that all measures taken for its conservation will be timely and effective." What a penultimate irony that the final and perhaps most intractable difficulty all these cats face may be their own magnificence and the reverence and awe in which we hold them.

The snow leopard, king of Shangri-La, has always been a shadowy, ephemeral presence due to the harsh and unforgiving places where it lives by killing other epic beasts who also thrive in the cold, thin air. If a committee of angels were convened to design an animal, the result might well look like the snow leopard and inhabit snow leopard country. We are just now coming to know and appreciate this legendary animal. Are we to lose him within the next human generation? ■

A snow leopard during the brief "easy time" of a high alpine summer.

Population Estimates

In October 1986, the landmark Fifth International Snow Leopard Symposium, sponsored by a number of parties including the government of India and the International Snow Leopard Trust (ISLT), was held in Srinagar, India. The papers from this meeting were published in 1988, and indicated the following estimates as of 1986:

Country	Estimated Minimum	Estimated Maximum
Afghanistan	unknown	unknown
Bhutan	unknown	unknown
China	350	350
(West Gansu)		
India	100	200
(Jammu and Kashmir)		
Mongolia	500	900
Nepal*	150	300
Pakistan	104	130
USSR	300	1,000
	1,504	2,880

*The above figures for Nepal were based on 1979 estimates by Rodney Jackson. By the mid-1980s, Jackson felt this estimate to be low. Also, at the time, the above figures were known to be crude, sometimes based on outdated estimates, and did not take into account large areas of China, the Himalayas, and the Hindu Kush Mountains.

Since then, these estimates have been revised upward to indicate that the world population of wild snow leopards is at least five thousand but probably does not exceed ten thousand. Mongolian and Polish wildlife specialists have since estimated Mongolia's snow leopard population at between two thousand and four thousand.

Much of the snow leopard's total range lies within China, and for political reasons it is not possible at this time to estimate total snow leopard numbers in that country. George Schaller indicated in the spring of 1988: "I would guess that at least 2,000 survive in the country."

Schaller also estimated in early 1990 that there were about two thousand snow leopards in Tibet, but that their numbers are declining. Eugene Koshkarev indicated in 1985 that the (now former) Soviet Union's estimated population of snow leopards had been upgraded from one thousand to two thousand. Populations in Pakistan and Afghanistan are known to be extremely low, due both to poaching and to shooting by military forces who fire at them at every opportunity.

As of December 31, 1988, snow leopards in captivity numbered 471 (243 males, and 228 females), an increase of 182 percent since 1976 when there were 167. There was a broad base of young animals, with 57 percent being under five years of age. There were thirty-seven potential founders—twenty-three males and fourteen females—animals caught in the wild who were without living descendants in the captive population. However, since all but seven were in China, experts are hoping for exchanges between North American zoos and those in China. ∎

Physical Characteristics
Size and Weight
The snow leopard's head and body length is thirty-eight to forty-eight inches (95–120cm), plus an additional thirty-two to thirty-five inches (80–88cm) for the long, well-furred tail, making for a total length of five and one-half to seven and one-half feet (1.7–2.3m). Its weight can vary from fifty-five pounds (25kg) for females to 165 pounds (74kg) for males, depending upon sex, season, condition of animal, and locale. Thus, the snow leopard is about the same size as the puma.

Pelage
The snow leopard's fur is thick and long, marked with black spots on the face, neck and legs, and with irregular circles on the back and flanks against a pale gray or pale gray-brown background. Its muzzle is short, its forehead high, and its chin vertical. In the winter, the fur is particularly long, dense, and woolly, with the hairs reaching one inch (2.5cm) on the back, two and one-half inches (6.25cm) on the belly, and two inches (5cm) on the tail. ■

Facing page: Magnificence in fur, even in summer fur. Note the long hind legs and the heavily furred tail which is curled around the cat for warmth when it lies down to rest in the severe winter weather. Right: A snow leopard comes to cool off in the summer when it can get very hot, even in the high mountain redoubts where this cat lives.

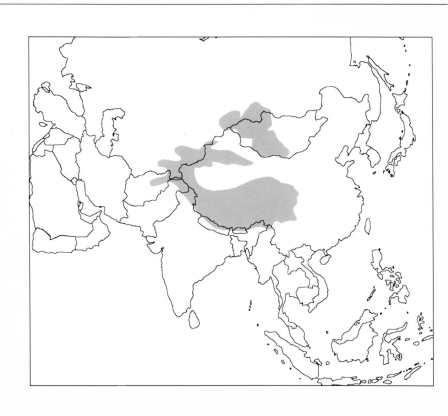

The Range of the
Snow Leopard
(*Panthera uncia*)

149

Above: *Snow leopards are extremely quick and athletic because agility is required to hunt successfully in the rough country that they frequent.* Left: *The Siberian ibex is tremendously nimble and inhabits some of the roughest, most broken country on earth. A worthy prey for the King of Shangri-La!*

Above: *In common with all other cats, snow leopards like to explore and hunt watercourses in their territories.* Left: *The markhor, king of the wild goat clan, lives in rough, broken country where only three or four other large animals could safely exist. One of those is the snow leopard!*

Known Habits of the Snow Leopard

This powerful and agile cat is often active during the day, especially at dawn and dusk. It hunts by stalking and ambushing prey, and then kills by strangling its quarry, as does the cheetah, which correlates well with the short, round canine teeth of both species.

Snow leopards radio-collared by Rodney Jackson, who has done extensive research on this animal since 1972, indicated that the snow leopard shows a marked preference for broken, rough country where the cat is better able to hide and stalk at close range and where its great agility may come more into play, as opposed to more open, level ground that would increase visibility and encourage longer chases. Where more level, even terrain was available, these cats still preferred to move along major ridgelines, bluff edges, and cliff bases or crests. All preferred steeper sites with cliffs among undulating slopes or broken terrain.

The snow leopard is, along with the puma, one of the most agile of all the big cats. C. Hart Merriam, a biologist known for his work in the American Southwest, mentioned in 1884 a puma that made a leap of sixty feet (18m) from a ledge twenty feet (6m) above

the ground, and another instance of a puma leaping nearly forty feet (12m) over snow. The snow leopard demonstrates comparable athletic ability. Russian researcher S. I. Ognev wrote in 1962 that the "Siberian [snow] leopard makes unbelievable leaps, and I would never have accepted stories about them if I had not seen them myself." Ognev added that he had witnessed a snow leopard leap over a ditch a distance of forty-nine feet (14.7m). Another jump of sixty feet (18m) has been recorded, but it was downhill and the angle of the slope was not recorded. Both pumas and snow leopards have been seen to jump to earth from trees or rocks fifty to sixty feet (15–18m) high and land on their feet apparently unhurt. Even though the typical leopard is approximately the same size, its stockier and more powerful body is not as supple, and no downward leaps of more than thirty feet (9m) (one that is documented was made out of a tree) are recorded for it in the literature. This is still a considerable achievement for an animal weighing more than one hundred pounds (45kg).

These are primarily solitary animals, but they are not asocial. There have been reports of groups of up to five hunting together, and of play between two adults. ■

Taxonomy of the Snow Leopard

Most authorities place the snow leopard in the genus *Panthera* with the great cats that roar: the lion, tiger, leopard, and jaguar. However, although snow leopards have been known to make a wide variety of vocalizations—grunting, meowing, moaning, growling, and hissing—they have never been known to roar. (For this and other reasons, a few taxonomists place them in their own genus, *Uncia*, naming the snow leopard *Uncia uncia*.) They are atypical of the pantherine cats in other ways, particularly the architecture of the skull, which is depressed at the top of a somewhat wide rostrum, rising to a broad, domed forehead, which accentuates the characteristic snubbed-nose look of this species. The expansion of the forehead is caused by an enlargement of the upper nasal chambers and sinuses. Researcher Theodor Haltenforth suggests this is a response to the snow leopard's extremely cold habitat.

Zoologist Nancy A. Neff has noted some similarities between the snow leopard and the cheetah, including long limbs relative to the length of the spine, some aspects of the shape of the skull, and details of the auditory region. Although it is a big cat, the snow leopard feeds in a crouched manner, as do the lesser cats. One Russian scientist has speculated that the Russian and Mongolian snow leopards should be accorded a separate subspecies as compared with those cats farther south in Nepal and other areas. However, this researcher had no specimens from the latter areas to support his thesis.

No subspecies of snow leopards have been named. ■

Below: *Just as that of many different species, the weight of a big cat can vary by season and by area. As a snow leopard goes into winter, it is in prime condition and at its heaviest weight. Coming out of winter, it is generally in a stressed condition and at its lightest. Also, animals with wide geographic distribution inevitably optimize in one or more areas and are marginal in others. The lower bounds of fifty-five pounds (25kg) would be for a female snow leopard from a small race or area, and 165 pounds (74kg) would be for a prime male in an optimum habitat.* Right: *A resting adult snow leopard, still surprisingly well-furred even in the summer heat.*

REFERENCES

ARTICLES AND PAPERS

Anderson, Allen E. February 1983. A critical review of literature on puma (Felis concolor). Special report no. 54, Colorado Department of Natural Resources, Division of Wildlife.

Bolgiano, Chris. May–June 1991. Texas' outcast cats. *Defenders.*

Brown, David E. January–February 1991. Revival for *El Tigre? Defenders.*

Brown, David E. May–June 1991. Looking for the Yuma Puma. *Defenders.*

Choudhary, Anwaruddin. July–September 1989. Tigers in India today. *Tiger Paper.* FAO Regional Office for Asia and the Pacific. Bangkok, Thailand.

Crawshaw, Peter G., Jr., and Quigley, Howard B. n.d. Jaguar spacing, activity, and habitat use in a seasonally flooded environment in Brazil. New York Zoological Society. New York, NY.

Dodd, G. H., and Squirrel, D. J. 1980. *Structure and mechanism in the mammalian olfactory system.* Symposium of the Zoological Society of London. vol. 45.

Emmons, Louise H. 1987. Comparative feeding ecology of felids in a neotropical rainforest. *Behavorial Ecology and Sociobiology.* Springer-Verlag.

Fitch-Snyder, Helen A. *Cheetah News.* Newsletter of the Zoological Society of San Diego. San Diego, CA.

Freeman, Helen. Oct. 1986. *Proceedings of the Fifth International Snow Leopard Symposium.* International Snow Leopard Trust and Wildlife Institute of India. Srinagar, India.

Hoogesteijn, Rafael; and Mondolfi, Edgardo; and Michelangeli, Armando. 1986. Conservation on the status of jaguar populations in Venezuela and its preservation rules. Proceedings of the International Council for Game and Wildlife Conservation and IUCN/SSC Ethnozoology Specialists Group, April 4–5, at Manaus, Brazil.

Hildebrand, M. Nov. 1959. Motions of the running cheetah and horse. *Journal of Mammalogy.* vol. 40, no. 4.

Hildebrand, M. May 1960. How animals run. *Scientific American.* vol. 202, no. 5.

Hildebrand, M. February 1961. Further studies on locomotion of the cheetah. *Journal of Mammalogy.* vol. 42, no. 1.

Houston, D. C. 1988. Digestive efficiency and hunting behavior in cats, dogs and vultures. *Journal of Zoology.* vol. 216. London, England.

IUCN. 1984. *The plight of the cats.* Proceedings of the meeting and workshop of the IUCN/SSC Cat Specialist Group, April 9–12, at Kanha National Park. Madhya Pradesh, India.

Jackson, Peter, ed. August 1989. A review by leopard specialists of *The status of leopard in sub-Saharan Africa* (Martin and de Meulenaer). IUCN/Cat Specialist Group. Gland, Switzerland.

Jackson, Peter, ed. *Cat News.* Newsletter of the Cat Specialist Group of the IUCN. Gland, Switzerland.

Johnson, Kurt A., and Franklin, William L. n.d. Ecology and management of the Patagonia puma (Felis concolor patagonica) in southern Chile. Iowa State University. Ames, Iowa.

Lindburg, Donald. March 1989. When cheetahs are kings. *ZooNooz.* San Diego Zoological Society. San Diego, CA.

Lumpkin, Susan. March–April 1991. Cats Special Issue. *Zoo Goer.* vol 20, no 2.

Marker, Laurie, and O'Brien, Stephen J. 1988. Captive breeding of the cheetah (Acinonyx jubatus) in North American zoos (1871–1986). *Zoo Biology.* vol. 8.

NOAHS Center. 1988. *International studbook/cheetah.* National Zoological Park. Washington, D.C.

Marker-Kraus, Laurie. n.d. *The North American cheetah species survival research master plan.* National Zoological Park, Smithsonian Institution. Washington, D.C.

Martin, R. B., and de Meulenaer, T. 1988. Survey of the status of the leopard (Panthera pardus) in Sub-Saharan Africa. Secretariat of the CITES. Lausanne, Switzerland.

Metha, Jai N., and Dhewaju, Ram Gopal. Jan.–March 1990. A note on the record of clouded leopards in Nepal. *Tiger Paper.* FAO Regional Office for Asia and the Pacific. Bangkok, Thailand.

Mills, M. G. L., et al. Some population characteristics of the lion (Panthera leo) in the Kalahari Gemsbok National Park. *Koedoe.* vol. 21.

Minnesota Zoological Garden. n.d. ISIS SDR abstract/mammals. Apple Valley, MN.

Myers, Norman. 1975. *The cheetah* (Acinonyx jubatus) *in Africa.* IUCN monograph. no. 4. Gland, Switzerland.

Naewboonnien, J., ed. *Tiger Paper.* FAO Regional Office for Asia and the Pacific. Bangkok, Thailand.

O'Brien, S. J., et al. March 22, 1985. Genetic basis for species vulnerability in the cheetah. *Science.* vol. 227.

O'Brien, Stephen J., and Wildt, David E. July 29, 1983. The cheetah is depauperate in genetic variation. *Science.* vol. 221, no. 4609.

Patnaik, S. K., and Acharijyo, L. N. January–March 1990. White tiger in India: its past and present. *Tiger Paper.* FAO Regional Office for Asia and the Pacific. Bangkok, Thailand.

Quigley, Howard B., and Crawshaw, Peter G., Jr. n.d. A conservation plan for the jaguar in the Panatal region of Brazil. New York Zoological Society. New York, NY.

Rind, Sherry, ed. *Snow Line.* Newsletter for the International Snow Leopard Trust. Seattle, WA.

Roberson, Jay, and Lindzey, Frederick. 1984. *Mountain lion: second workshop proceedings.* Zion National Park. Springdale, UT.

Russell, Dennis N. *History and status of felids in Texas.* 1971. Texas Parks and Wildlife Dept. Austin, TX.

Sanchez-Arino, Tony. Winter 1990. The great man-eaters. *Game Coin Bulletin.* San Antonio, TX.

Santiapillai, Charles. March 1987. Clouded leopard in Sumatra. *Cat News.* vol. 6.

Santiapillai, Charles. January–March 1989. The status and conservation of the clouded leopard (Neofelis nebulosa diardi) in Sumatra. *Tiger Paper.* FAO Regional Office for Asia and the Pacific. Bangkok, Thailand.

Seal, Ulysses S. *CBSG News.* Newsletter of the Captive Breeders Specialty Group, IUCN Species Survival Commission. Gland, Switzerland.

Smith, Ronald H., ed. December 6–8, 1988. *Proceedings of the third mountain lion workshop.* Arizona chapter of the Wildlife Society, Arizona Fish and Game Dept. Prescott, AZ.

Swank, Wendell G., and Teer, James G. January 1989. Status of the jaguar. *Oryx.* vol. 23, no 1.

Tewes, Michael. *Cat Conservation Newsletter.* Newsletter of the Feline Research Program, Caesar Kleberg Wildlife Research Institute. Texas A & I University. Kingsville, TX.

Tilson, Ronald L., and Binczik, G. Allen. *Tiger Beat.* Newsletter of the Tiger Species Survival Plan. Minnesota Zoo. Apple Valley, MN.

Wildland Management Center School of Natural Resources. July 1985. First jaguar preserve in the Americas. *Endangered Species Technical Bulletin* reprint. University of Michigan. vol. 2, no. 9.

Van Aarde, R. J., and Van Dyk, Ann. 1986. Inheritance of the king coat colour pattern in cheetahs (Acinonyx jubatus). Zoological Society of London. vol. 209. London, England.

BOOKS

Amin, Mohamid, and Eames, John, eds. *Insight Guides: Kenya*. Hong Kong: APA Productions, 1987.

Ammann, Katherine and Karl. *Cheetah*. New York: Arco Publishing, 1985.

Bauer, Erwin A. *Predators of North America*. Harrisburg, PA: Outdoor Life/ Stackpole Books, 1988.

Bandino, Guido. *The Big Cats*. London: Orbis Publishing, 1975.

Bedi, Ramesh, and Bedi, Rajesh. *Indian Wildlife*. New Delhi, India: Brijbasi Printers Private Ltd., 1984.

Beard, Peter Hill. *The End of the Game*. London: Paul Hamlyn, 1985

Bertram, Brian. *Pride of Lions*. New York: Charles Scribner's Sons, 1978.

Bond, Creina; Johnson, Peter; and Bannister, Anthony. *Okavango: Sea of Land, Land of Water*. Cape Town and Johannesburg, South Africa: C. Struik Publishers, 1977.

Duggan, Alan, ed. *Readers' Digest Illustrated Guide to the Game Parks and Nature Reserves of Southern Africa*. Cape Town: Readers' Digest Association of South Africa (Pty) Ltd., 1983.

Dyer, Anthony, and Kuhn, Bob. *Classic African Animals: The Big Five*. New York: Winchester Press, 1973.

Eaton, Randall L. *The Cheetah: The Biology, Ecology, and Behavior of an Endangered Species*. Malabar, Florida: Robert E. Krieger Publishing, 1974.

Ewer, R. F. *The Carnivores*. Ithaca, New York: Comstock Publishing Associates, Cornell University Press, 1973.

Frame, George and Lory. *Swift and Enduring: Cheetahs and Wild Dogs of the Serengeti*. New York: E. P. Dutton, 1981.

Gittleman, John L., ed. *Carnivore Behavior, Ecology, and Evolution*. Ithaca, New York: Comstock Publishing Assoc., Cornell University Press, 1989.

Gordeon, Rene, and Bannister, Anthony. *The National Parks of South Africa*. Cape Town and Johannesburg, South Africa: C. Struik Publishers.

Grobler, Hans; Hall-Martin, Anthony; and Walker, Clive. *Predators of Southern Africa*. Johannesburg, South Africa: MacMillan South Africa (Pty) Ltd., 1984.

Guggisberg, C. A. W. *Wild Cats of the World*. New York: Taplinger Publishing Co., 1975.

Gurung, K. K. *Heart of the Jungle: The Wildlife of Chitwan, Nepal*. London: Andre Deutsch Ltd. and Tiger Tops, 1983.

Hingston, R. W. G. *The Meaning of Animal Colour and Adornment*. London: Edward Arnold, 1933.

Israel, Samuel, and Sinclair, Toby, editors. *Insight Guides: Indian Wildlife*. Hong Kong: APA Productions, 1987.

Jackman, Brian, and Scott, Jonathan. *The Marsh Lions: The Story of an African Pride*. Boston: David R. Godine Publisher, 1983.

Jackson, Peter. *Endangered Species: Tigers*. Secaucus, NJ: Chartwell Books, 1990.

Kingdon, Johnathan. *East African Mammals: An Atlas of Evolution in Africa*. vol. III, *Carnivores*. Chicago: University of Chicago Press, 1977.

Kitchener, Andrew. *The Natural History of Wild Cats*. Ithaca, New York: Comstock Publishing Associates, Cornell University Press, 1991.

Luard, Nicholas. *The Wildlife Parks of Africa*. London: Michael Joseph, 1985.

Martin, Paul S., and Klein, Richard G., eds. *Quaternary Extinctions: A Prehistoric Revolution*. Tucson, AZ: University of Arizona Press, 1989.

McDougal, C. *The Face of the Tiger*. London: Rivington Books/Andre Deutsch, 1977.

Miller, S. Douglas, and Everett, Daniel D., eds. *Cats of the World: Biology, Conservation, and Management*. Washington, D.C.: Caesar Kleberg Wildlife Research Institute and National Wildlife Foundation, 1986.

Mills, Gus, and Haagner, Clem. *Guide to the Kalahari Gemsbok National Park*. Johannesburg, South Africa: Southern Book Publishers (Pty) Ltd., 1989.

Moss, Cynthia. *Portraits in the Wild: Animal Behavior in East Africa*. Chicago: University of Chicago Press, 1982.

Mountfort, Guy, and Cubitt, Gerald. *Wild India: The Wildlife and Scenery of India and Nepal*. London: Collins, 1985.

Myers, Norman. *The Cheetah (Acinonyx jubatus) in Africa*. Morges, Switzerland: IUCN Mongraph No. 4., International Union for the Conservation of Nature and Natural Resources, 1975.

Myers, Norman. *The Leopard (Panthera pardus) in Africa*. Morges, Switzerland: IUCN Monograph No. 5., International Union for the Conservation of Nature and Natural Resources, 1976.

Own, Denis. *Grasslands of Africa*. New York: The National Audubon Society/Franklin Library, 1981.

Paynter, David, and Nussey, Wilf. *Kruger: Portrait of a National Park*. Johannesburg, South Africa: MacMillan South Africa (Pty) Ltd., 1986.

Perry, R. *The World of the Jaguar*. New York: Taplinger, 1970.

Prater, S. H. *The Book of Indian Animals*. Bombay, India: Bombay Natural History Society, 1965.

Rabinowitz, Alan. *Chasing the Dragon's Tail: The Struggle to Save Thailand's Wild Cats*. New York: Doubleday, 1991.

Rabinowitz, Alan. *Jaguar: One Man's Battle to Establish the World's First Jaguar Preserve*. New York: Doubleday, 1991.

Rathore, Fateh Singh, et al. *With Tigers in the Wild: An Experience in an Indian Forest*. New Delhi, India: Vikas Publishing House, Pvt., Ltd., 1983.

Sales, G., and Pye, D. *Ultrasonic Communication by Animals*. London: Chapman & Hall, 1974.

Sankhala, Kailash. *Tiger: The Story of the Indian Tiger*. London: Collins, 1978.

Schaller, George B. *The Deer and the Tiger: A Study of Wildlife in India*. Chicago and London: University of Chicago Press, 1984.

Schaller, George B. *The Serengeti Lion: A Study of Predator-Prey Relations*. Chicago and London: University of Chicago Press, 1976.

Scott, Jonathan. *The Leopard's Tale*. London: Elm Tree Books, 1985.

Server, Lee. *Tigers: A Look into the Glittering Eye*. New York: W. H. Smith, Ltd., 1991.

Shaw, Harley. *Soul among Lions: The Cougar as Peaceful Adversary*. Boulder, CO: Johnson Books, 1989.

Shuker, Karl P. N. *Mystery Cats of the World: From Blue Tigers to Exmoor Beasts*. London: Robert Hale, 1989.

Sinclair, A. R. E., and Norton-Griffiths, M., eds. *Serengeti: Dynamics of an Ecosystem*. Chicago and London, University of Chicago Press, 1979.

Singh, Arjan. *Prince of Cats*. New Delhi: B. I. Publications, and London: Jonathan Cape, 1982.

Singh, Arjan. *Tara-a Tigress*. London: Quartet Books, Ltd., 1981.

Singh, Arjan. *Tiger! Tiger!* London: Jonathan Cape, 1984.

Smithers, Reay H. N. *The Animals of the Southern African Subregion*. Pretoria, South Africa: University of Pretoria, 1983.

Smuts, G. L. *Lion*. Johannesburg, South Africa: MacMillan South Africa (Pty) Ltd., 1982.

Stuart, Chris and Tilde. *Field Guide to the Mammals of Southern Africa*. Cape Town, South Africa: Struik, 1988.

Thapar, Valmik. *Tiger: Portrait of a Predator*. New York: Facts on File Publications, 1986.

Thapar, Valmik, and Rathore, Fateh Singh. *Tigers: The Secret Life*. Emmaus, PA: Rodale Press, 1989.

Tilson, Ronald L., and Seal, Ulysses S., eds. *Tigers of the World: The Biology, Biopolitics, Management, and Conservation of an Endangered Species*. Park Ridge, NJ: Noyes Publications, 1987.

Wood, Gerald L. *The Guiness Book of Animal Facts and Feats*. Middlesex, U.K.: Enfield.

Young, Stanley P., and Goldman, Edward A. *The Puma: Mysterious American Cat*. New York: Dover Publications, 1946.

Ziesler, Gunter, and Hofer, Angelika. *Safari: The East African Diaries of a Wildlife Photographer*. New York: Facts on File Publications, 1984.

Zur Strassen, Helmut. *Etosha Image: Southwest Africa*. Cape Town, Johannesburg, London: Purnell, 1974.

INDEX

PHOTOGRAPHER'S NOTES

The technologies relating to cameras, optics, and films are expanding at an exponential rate, creating a veritable revolution in wildlife photography within the last five years alone. During this period, the explosion of new capabilities has seen many of the old icons either superseded or smashed outright.

Professional wildlife photographers shoot color positive (slide) films for reproduction, not color negative (print) films. For thirty years or more, Kodak's Kodachrome was the wildlife film of choice worldwide due to its fine grain and beautiful color. Because the photos in this book were shot over a twenty-year period, most of them were shot on either Kodachrome II or Kodachrome 64.

However, in recent years, several marvelous new E-6 type films, most notably Fuji Velvia and Fujichrome 100, have shouldered Kodachrome aside with their brighter (some traditionalists say gaudy) colors and the superb fine grain of Velvia. As this is being written, Kodak is introducing its own new generation of E-6 transparency films, which are designated as Ektachrome Lumiere films. These films *finally* incorporate Kodak's T-GRAIN technology in all three color layers. This T-GRAIN technology has been available in assorted Kodak black-and-white films for years now, and its fine-grained sharpness is a great benefit.

Although I do not speak for any of the film makers, it does seem readily apparent that Kodak has decided to treat further development of Kodachrome with "benign neglect," while they pour all their R&D into a head-to-head E-6 vs. E-6 battle with Fuji. This may or may not be a wise decision. There is still one undeniable advantage, for some of us, that Kodachrome offers over any of the E-6 films extant to date from Kodak, Fuji, or any other maker.

Kodachrome is actually a black and white film (no color dyes in the film itself) with the color being added, as "coded" by the film, during an exceedingly complex bath process in the lab. All the E-6 films, on the other hand, carry the color dyes right in the film itself, making for much simpler lab processing and thus faster turnaround and more convenience generally for the user.

However, the fact that there is no color dye in the film itself makes Kodachrome a very stable film that can tolerate horrific abuse by heat and humidity. All too often I have had to carry or leave both exposed and unexposed film in vehicles that promptly turned into pressure cookers because of tropic heat. Obviously, I tried to guard against this and never let it happen unless completely unavoidable. However, if you carry very large amounts of film and do so in strange and exotic places, it is all too often simply unavoidable. I have never had Kodachrome degrade on me. Not once.

For just as many years as Kodachrome was ascendant, Nikon was the world standard among professional-grade, top-of-the-marque 35mm camera systems. Most of the photos in this book were shot with assorted Nikon F2's, F3's, and F4's. Nikon is still a very fine camera system and arguably remains the best in the world. However, Canon has been more aggressive in bringing new technology on-stream for the last ten years, and they have largely managed to do it while maintaining very high standards of quality and durability. They are, quite literally, giving professional photographers "more firepower." For this reason, after twenty years as a dedicated Nikon user, I switched to Canon last year. I have not been sorry that I did so.

Most of us in the current "mature" generation of U.S. wildlife still photographers are more or less self-taught in things-technical. We generally came to wildlife photography through an abiding interest in the animals, not through any informed expertise in photography. Often we started off as hunters (those were radically different times) and evolved into something else. Inevitably, this human profile is changing as many of the fine young wildlife photographers break into the field with differing origins and histories. These young photographers are producing work that is often absolutely astonishing in both its technical virtuosity and its esthetic point of view.

Wildlife photography is immensely rewarding on a personal level. I cannot think of anything I would rather do. ■

ABOUT THE AUTHOR

Photo by Jeanne Drake

TOM BRAKEFIELD has been a full-time freelance wildlife photographer and writer for the past twenty years. His articles and photographs have appeared in leading books, magazines, and newspapers throughout the world. He is the author of five previous books.

During the course of his travel and work, Brakefield has been fascinated by many families of animals ranging from the bears, primates, whales, canids, pachyderms, and birds to many of the smaller, not so grand species. But, as he readily admits, the predators have always particularly captivated him, especially the big cats.

Home for Brakefield is Hendersonville, Tennessee, in the midst of more than two hundred different Japanese maples, dwarf conifers, and other exotic trees from around the world. Their beauty and longevity lend some solace in a world that seems destined to allow no wild place for the big cats on a long-term basis. ■

Foreword writer **ALAN SHOEMAKER** has held the position of Curator of Mammals at the Riverbanks Zoological Park in Columbia, South Carolina, since 1989, although he has been with the zoo since 1972. The author of over sixty professional and scientific publications, Shoemaker was appointed the International Studbook Keeper for rare leopards maintained in captivity in 1974. In 1983 he was appointed to the IUCN/SSC Cat Specialist Committee, becoming Deputy Chair in 1991. ■

Above: Tom Brakefield emerges from a steamy forest in central India after a long day of chasing tigers with a camera. Overleaf: The queen at her table. An adult lioness in Botswana dines off a nearly-adult Cape buffalo that she has helped to kill. It takes a highly trained pride to bring down such large, powerful prey.